This book belongs to

_____

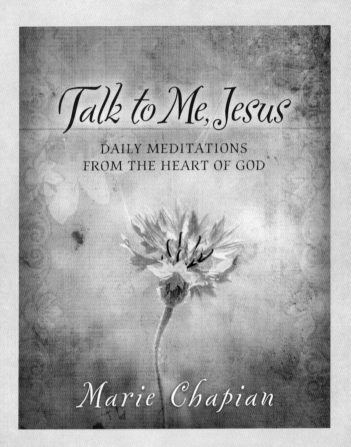

Talk to Me, Jesus

DAILY MEDITATIONS
FROM THE HEART OF GOD

Marie Chapian

BroadStreet
P U B L I S H I N G

BroadStreet Publishing Group LLC.
Racine, Wisconsin, USA
Broadstreetpublishing.com

Talk to Me, Jesus: Daily Meditations from the Heart of God

© 2015 Marie Chapian

ISBN 978-1-4245-4962-7 (hard cover)
ISBN 978-1-4245-5011-1 (e-book)

Design by Chris Garborg | www.garborgdesign.com
Editorial services by Michelle Winger | www.literallyprecise.com

Printed in China.

17 18 19 20 21   7 6 5 4 3 2

In the morning, LORD,

you hear my voice;

in the morning I lay

my requests before you

and wait expectantly.

PSALM 5:3, NIV

INTRODUCTION

THROUGHOUT THE SCRIPTURES JESUS YEARNS
FOR HIS CHILDREN TO HEAR HIS VOICE AND
ENTER A DEEPLY INTIMATE RELATIONSHIP
WITH HIM. THIS LITTLE BOOK OF SCRIPTURE-
BASED WORDS OF JESUS WILL HELP BRING YOU
INTO A CLOSER WALK WITH THE ONE WHO
LOVES YOU WITH AN EVERLASTING LOVE.
EACH AND EVERY DAY OF THE YEAR WHEN
YOU OPEN YOUR HEART TO HIS, YOU'LL FIND
A SPECIAL WORD WAITING FOR YOU TO LIFT
YOU UP, ENCOURAGE YOU, GUIDE YOU, AND
DELIGHT YOU THROUGHOUT YOUR WHOLE
DAY. HE'S DRAWING YOU INTO HIS LOVING
EMBRACE 365 DAYS A YEAR.
MAY HIS WORDS PERMEATE YOUR LIFE ALL
YEAR LONG AND FOR YEARS TO COME...

JANUARY

In the beginning was the Word,
and the Word was with God,
and the Word was God.

JOHN 1:1, NIV

January 1

I'm your mountain of strength for your new year.
I'm your mighty mountain, lofty and majestic;
I'm your mountain of awesome power and might.
I bend down at the sound of your cry.
I stoop to lift you out of danger. I pull you out
of the miry pit of wrong choices. I wipe away
the splotches and smudges of every past mistake.
I make all things new.

Don't fall prey to the foolishness of envy and pride.
Blessing after blessing will come to you
when you trust Me. I'm all you need.

PSALM 40:1-4; PROVERBS 13:10

January 2

Don't fret transition and reverse plans,
for these are gifts to stretch your faith.
I'm your provider.
I'm the God of all there is,
and I tell you not to underestimate
My power and authority
in every situation concerning you.
Never fear the unexpected
and the unpredictable;
never stagger at the thought of change.
I provide everything you need
and much more.

PSALM 23:1; DEUTERONOMY 8:7-14;
PHILIPPIANS 4:19

January 3

Don't look back. Never look back.

Keep your eyes fixed on the dawn.

I rise *in you* every morning

and in the gold of daybreak, I slip your burdens

beneath the beauty of My overcoming love.

Will you look for My smile to dispel your hurt feelings?

I want to fill the vacant places in your soul.

Will you allow My arms to hold you

so you'll stay on track?

Will you allow My grace to sustain you

so you won't continue muttering self-defeating words

to yourself?

Will you allow My joy to fortify your spirit?

I've hidden you in Me.

I don't leave you for a single moment.

My eye is always upon you.

Isaiah 41:10, 60:1, 61:3; Jeremiah 29:11;
2 Corinthians 12:9; Proverbs 5:21

January 4

Listen for Me in unexpected places–
Yes, listen for Me
in the sound of a fluttering bird,
in the wail of the wind,
the groan of traffic,
and in the sound of a cell phone
crying in your pocket.

Hear Me in the spill of night
when the world sleeps
and My children breathe the kisses of angels.
Hear Me when you cough and blow your nose
while reaching for a glass of water;
hear Me when I tenderly hold your darling head
in My hands,
and hum a healing love song in your ear.

PSALM 29:4; EXODUS 18:19; JEREMIAH 31:3

January 5

Your safety is in Me. I'm your refuge.
In the shadow of My wings I keep you safe
where no harm can reach you.
If you wear the strangling girdle of stress
you become the shape of stress.
If you wear the cloak of worry,
you take on its shape,
and if you dance in the shoes
of distress and panic,
the band leaves the room
and grabs health and happiness
on the way out.
What will you choose today?

Psalm 57:1; Proverbs 10:15-17; John 14:27;
Matthew 11:28-30

January 6

It's strength and courage you need today.
I'm giving you the power
to forge ahead
with joy and holy determination.
Be strong!
I'm giving you freedom
from the forces that have kept you
from moving full tilt
toward your divine destiny.

Take *big steps* today, and push through
the obstacles and hindrances
that have been thorns in your flesh.
I'm in you and right beside you.
I'm empowering you
to shake the dust from your hair
and make that hurdle
into victory *now*.

JOSHUA 1:9; PHILIPPIANS 3:12-15;
COLOSSIANS 1:10-12; EPHESIANS 6:10; 1 JOHN 5:4

January 7

Love Me enough to desire
what I desire for you.
When you dash off on your own,
you're like one dying of thirst and running
the wrong way for water.
I'm your Savior and your Friend.
I'm the oasis in the desert
and your heavenly supply.
Honor Me by pausing to learn about My wants
and desires for you. This is how you become
a living prayer.

Psalm 63:1-3; Revelation 21:6

January 8

When your soul is stirred with a longing
you can't identify, and your heart beats
in a pattern that tells you something's missing,
retreat for a moment to make space
for your gift of creativity.
I've gifted you with a creative soul
and you must make space for your inner
longings to find expression.

Oh, so many ways to release the gifts
I've placed in you! Listen intimately
to the world around you and to the dimensions of
My divine presence.
I've gifted you with the ability to see
beneath the surface of things
and to give voice to your unique vision and
passion. Your life is the exuberant arena
of the gifts I've given you. Allow your gifts to unfold
and richly flow.
Today, allow yourself to flourish!

PHILIPPIANS 1:9; PSALM 107:9; MATTHEW 7:11;
2 CORINTHIANS 4:15

January 9

Today, I'm giving you a new perspective
so you'll see things through My eyes.
I want you to see the view from *My* window.
Rub My salve of holy vision
on your human eyes, and the blurred sight
and darkness will fall off you
like a heavy drape flopping to the ground.
You'll begin to understand yourself
and your role in My ultimate purpose.
If you could see what I see
you'd never grind your teeth, fidget, fret,
or lose a minute of sweet peaceful sleep.
To see clearly is to understand. You've eaten
the honey of My Word, tasted the blessings
of My favor, and now I'm giving you
new sight. The higher you step up to Me
the clearer the vision and the further you'll see.

EPHESIANS 1:18

January 10

I lift from you now every false burden and
feeling of heaviness
that tries to surround you.
I remove the sluggish warp of oppression
that seeks to overwhelm you.
No depression will capture your heart
and mind. You're free to see the truth
of every situation from My point-of-view.
I prohibit and halt every droopy, self-absorbed
preoccupation that comes near you.
Take your power today and stand against all
demonic threats to your happiness and
contentment in My name.
My Holy Spirit will sweetly
and beautifully flow through your emotions
when you cast every care on Me!
I'll transform your mind
to be able to see and anticipate
the wondrous things
I've planned for you.

ISAIAH 54:14; 1 PETER 5:7; PSALM 32:7;
JEREMIAH 29:11

January 11

I've given you many gifts.
Show your creative side today.
Think how I can create something
astonishingly beautiful from ashes,
and how I transform mourning into joy–
think how I dress you up in garments
of praise for your spirit of heaviness.
The gladness I wrap you in lathers you
with a precious healing ointment.
I'm the creator of all things on earth and in heaven,
and I've given you
creative gifts to express Myself through you.
Be free today to fully express your gifts
in a flurry of love and delight,
and praise Me for your creativity
which I want you to wear like a kingly robe.

Isaiah 61:3; Psalm 147:1; John 8:36

January 12

Dear one, I haven't sent you out alone.
No, no no, never alone.
I'm right beside you, and My Spirit
goes before you preparing every millimeter
of your way. Never think you're alone even
when the way bristles with the unknown,
and danger snarls in the shadows.
I'm your courage! Not only that,
I'm the light that exposes the pests of the soul,
those ruinous thoughts that tell you you're alone.

Tell yourself today you're *never* alone.
The unredeemed in their self-pity
may distress themselves with loneliness,
but you're endowed with wisdom and
a creative spirit, and these are your friends.
You're not alone. Never, never, never.

DEUTERONOMY 31:8; JOHN 8:12; EXODUS 15:2;
PSALM 107:14; MATTHEW 28:20

January 13

I'm a God of surprises.
I love to usher new events
and situations into your life that
inspire you to dig deeper
into My Word–situations that
cause you to drop your habits
of complacency and seek Me
on a deeper level.
I'm calling you to see with My eyes,
to think with My mind.
Dear one, there's no problem
you'll ever face in your life
that My Word doesn't cover.

JUDGES 6:11-16; ISAIAH 55:8-9;
HEBREWS 10:38

January 14

I fight your battles and settle your scores.
I work out solutions with those
who contend with you.
Let *others* contend, but *you* don't contend.
Hold your peace and listen for wisdom very attentively.
Wisdom's instructions are not always
the same or as you might expect.
I tell you, there's a time to make peace
and a time to take arms,
a time to break down and a time to build up,
a time to rip out and a time to mend.

Listen for Wisdom's guidance in such a time as this.
I'm here to protect you as the enemy creeps hungrily about
eager to devour all in his path.
Your enemy is not human, dear one, and you won't escape
with your feeble human tactics and devices.
I tell you, no weapon formed against you
will prosper because you're Mine,
so I ask you to let Me take charge of the battles.

ECCLESIASTES 3:1-8; JOB 33:33; ISAIAH 54:17

January 15

Listen. I want you to hear My voice at all times.
I want to be able to speak to you at any hour of the day
or night and know you'll listen. My heart holds
a heavenly kingdom of wisdom, love, and joy to share with you.
If you'll listen.
The way to listen is with your heart.
The thoughts from My heart to yours will ignite in you–
a mighty brightness that could light up the whole world.
I've called you to be this beacon of light,
fixed and permeating through every storm
and even through the blackest and starless of nights.

Listen. I'm teaching you to discern what is true and honorable
and worthy of your attention. I'm showing you what to revere,
what things are noble, reputable, authentic, pure, and lovely.
Listen. I'm showing you the beauty of meditating on the best,
not the worst; the beautiful, not the ugly; things to praise,
not things to curse;
and how to love as I love.

Exodus 18:19; Luke 11:36; Philippians 4:8;
1 John 4:7-8

January 16

I speak to you day and night.
I love to tell you things, teach you,
help you, guide you.
I'm your Lord and your life, and
when you live in My will for you,
all you touch your hand to
will radiate with the presence and the kiss
of the Almighty.
But without Me go ahead and cradle
jeweled cities in your sleeves, dine in banquet halls
with governors and kings,
and all will perish.
Poof.
Without *Me* you can do nothing!
Live in Me, snuggled vitally united to Me,
for this is your sure path to understanding who you are
and what you are called to do in this life.
Why do I tell you this?
Because we're *one.* Always, always, always
remember this.

John 10:15, 27, 15:4-5; Psalm 32:8; John 17:22

January 17

Your true home is safely settled
in My heart,
for this is where you were born to live.
Fear and worry will always
choke the happiness you were born to possess.
Beloved, in Me there's absolutely *no* fear.
Nothing rattles Me—nothing!
I'm all peace and all joy. I'm contentment,
and I'm *happy*. I've promised you My peace,
and I've also told you I'd give you My take
on the things that bother you. You have *My mind*.
My mind is at ease!
I want you to be happy in the home
I've prepared for you on earth,
but recognize and fully grasp
that your real home is nestled inside My heart.

Psalms 91:1, 128:2, 144:15; Job 24:23; 1 John 4:18;
Jeremiah 15:16; 1 Corinthians 2:16

January 18

If you make your home with Me
and if our relationship
is intimate and organic,
and if I've made My home in you
and My words are at home in you,
how can I resist your requests?
Live and thrive in Me and you'll
succeed in your endeavors.
If you live obeying My voice
and loving Me, I'm in your plans!
I'm here guiding and directing you!
Your soul burgeons with increase
as you make your home in Me,
and that's why I've told you to ask
whatever you will
and it'll be done for you.
This is My promise to you.
Everything about you is important to Me.
Believe this.

John 14:23, 15:1-10, Mark 11:24; Joshua 1:8

January 19

You have My unmerited favor, and you're saved
from the judgment of others.
Don't allow fault finding to come near you.
Kick aside all condemning words
and notions. Remember, you're your worst critic,
so don't be swift to jump into the garbage bag
of guilt when it's unmerited. I've tucked you into My heart
and your life is new and beautiful, replete with
healing and wisdom. Guilt has no hold on you!
I've set you free with My delicious
forgiveness.
I've given you goodness and mercy as partners.
They follow you all the days of your life.
Favor, dear one, includes My love song
that doesn't miss a note. I've called you
to increase in favor, so enjoy the song,
dance in your freedom.
Love who you are.

Job 10:12; 1 Kings 4:29; Proverbs 7:18

January 20

Living in Me, vitally united to Me
is the key to wisdom and understanding
of My omnipotent mind.
When you ingest the words I speak
to you; when you meditate and ponder
what I tell you,
a new power takes shape in your spirit.
The authority of My words
bubble up in you to give you wisdom,
discretion, and understanding.
I see your situation now.
My Word will guide and instruct you.
Never succumb to confusion.
You have My Word in you.

Psalm 18:30; Isaiah 58:11; John 16:13

January 21

Are you in need of a new vision for your life?
Are you longing for change?
If so, quiet your heart now
and withdraw into the stillness of the hour,
undisturbed by outside influences
and interferences.
Be still and calmly concentrate
on the presence of the Father.
Your desires are seeds for you to nourish
because you were born with more
than one purpose. As you quiet yourself
in prayer before the throne of grace,
listen for the guidance of My Holy Spirit,
wait for the anointing of your Savior,
and the perfect will of My Father
will be made clear.

Psalms 4:46, 32:8, 46:10; Luke 1:79; John 16:13

January 22

I free you from all your fears.
Join your life with Mine afresh this day
and expect unique, extraordinary blessings
and opportunities to come your way. I'll move
mightily on your behalf as you trust Me.
Look! All things are new in your life
and the fears of the past are gone
because you're a new person today.
I've given you a fresh start.
Come, let's be happy together
as you plunge forward
on the fabulous road ahead.

2 CORINTHIANS 5:17; DEUTERONOMY 1:21;
PROVERBS 16:20

January 23

I've delivered you from
your patterns of wrong thinking
and your old
self-destructive habits
and given you a new mind-set.
The traps of the past are shattered
and done away with.
You're altogether new!
Your beautiful brain now forms
fresh, inspiring, and revelatory truths,
so you'll bring life and light
into situations that were once too confusing
and disarming for you.
Your changed thinking patterns
are no longer stained
with the world's sad stab at enlightenment,
and you're going to prevail
in all things!

Colossians 3:2; Ephesians 4:23; Isaiah 61:7;
John 8:31-32, 36; 2 Samuel 22:19

January 24

I love your curiosity
and your throbbing interest
in the world I've created.
I delight with you as you appreciate
with awe My creation.
Because of your holy enthusiasm,
I'll show you much, much more to love.
I'll give you My holy microscope,
and you'll learn more
of the subtleties of My hand.

No branch or tree is voiceless,
no rock without a song of praise.
Can you feel the heartbeat of a stone, a leaf,
or dove? Can you hear
My furtive breath in a gentle snowfall?
I've given you the world
to care for, to be fruitful in and multiply.
Be glad in what I've given you.
I created it all for you.

GENESIS 1:28-31, 2:15

January 25

Be still.

You're strongest when you're still.

In quietness and confidence you're strong.

I'm with you and I'm the LORD

who is exalted above all the earth!

I hold you in the palm of My hand.

You're safe here and *now*.

This moment

is your safe place, for I am your safe place.

No need to fight your own battles.

No need to rush out to defend yourself.

Your personal arsenal of weapons

are pockets of lint–weightless and wearisome.

No ground is ever gained

with your emotional attempts without Me.

When I'm beside you, the battle is won.

I'm your fierce and undefeated weapon.

ISAIAH 30:15; PSALM 46:10-11;
2 CHRONICLES 20:17

January 26

I'm the source of all wisdom,
and your natural reasoning
will lead you astray.
Remember, nothing is hidden
from My eyes.
I see the challenges that you face today
and I'm taking care of all that concerns you.
Be attentive to obey the promptings of My Spirit;
resist the temptation to hotly
go forth in your own strength in matters
too great for you to handle without Me.
When you're spiritually flexible and obedient;
when you are patient and submissive
to My leading,
you'll see miracles.
Miracles, I tell you!
I can change a situation
in the flicker of an eye
and without Me, you cannot.

John 15:5; Isaiah 1:19; Job 12:13; Psalm 51:6;
James 4:7; Galatians 3:5

January 27

Give the tears of the past to Me
and I'll empty them into the Sea of Deference.
Tears, like blades scratching stone,
will no longer carve the flesh of your cheeks.
The past is finished with its hot tears
and its heckling pain. Ashes have no life and are
good for nothing. Don't sit in the ashes
of yesterday's sorrow when I've crushed them
beneath the promises of My Word.

Trample on sorrow today,
for your battle scars are numbered in heaven.
Nothing escapes heaven's watchful eye, and
with one breath I defeat your enemies.
Defer them to Me,
all of them.

Song of Songs 2:11; 2 Peter 1:9; Isaiah 61:3,
60:20; Romans 8:37

January 28

I want to give you a holy microscope to learn
of the subtle thrills of life in My Spirit.
I want you to look deep and long enough
into My Word to see the blessings I have for you.
There are no tears in any corner
of heaven, beloved. Defer yours to Me and *whoosh*,
they're plunged into the sea of deference.
I'm setting you free from the captive claws of worry
and the dark emotions that pull
and snap at you. As you've sown in tears
you'll now reap with joy.
Be receptive to My voice and grasp
My immutable promise of holy *joy*.
I want you to see the great things
I'm doing for you today.

PSALMS 30:5, 126:5; ISAIAH 25:8, 60:20;
NEHEMIAH 8:10

January 29

The past is over and gone
and you're on a new path now.
I forgive you, dear one,
so you ought to forgive yourself.
It's good to turn from a self-toward
habitual way of life and ask forgiveness.
Receive My forgiveness plus the blessing
of a clean slate and refreshed spirit
When you're fed up with and finished
with self-centered worries and concerns,
you'll begin to truly *live the good life*!
You'll experience clean, beautiful
joyous freedom in Me because your eyes
will be open to increased hope and faith,
and you'll have so much satisfaction–
great enough to *forgive yourself.*
All is new, fresh, flawless, and wonderful!
I love you.

Hebrews 8:12, 10:22; Philippians 4:7; Micah 7:18;
Acts 26:18; Song of Songs 2:11; Romans 8:1;
2 Corinthians 5:17; 1 Peter 5:6-7

January 30

Every step you take, you take with Me
at your side.
When you are weary or uncertain,
I pick you up and carry you
in My arms.
If you're more passionate about
what goes wrong in life than you are for
what is beautiful and blessed,
you'll attract more of the same.
Come. Relax in the perfume
of My Holy Spirit's breath
on your cheek.
For too long you've thought of Me
as distant and aloof,
but I've never ever been distant
and aloof. That is a wrong concept
of Me. Look up, dear one.
I'm right here.
Right now. With you.
Always.

PROVERBS 23:7; MATTHEW 28:20

January 31

I go ahead of you and gift you
with blessings
before they're even a thought
in your head.
I answer needs you haven't even
asked for. I give you riches
you have no name for.
My thoughts are so much higher
than yours, and that's why today
it's necessary for you to ask
what's best for *Me* in your current situation.
I've promised to supply over and above
everything you need, and when praying
for what is best for *Me* and My kingdom
in all things pertaining to you,
you'll always have what is best for *you*.

1 KINGS 3:13; PSALMS 23:5; 40:51; JEREMIAH 29:11;
MATTHEW 6:33

FEBRUARY

"Speak, for Your servant is listening."

1 SAMUEL 3:10, NASB

February 1

Make more space to unleash
your creative powers today.
Allow yourself to move more freely
in your daily life.
Routine is good, but be aware that
dullness can agitate you.
A fixed routine offering no challenge
can stifle you, and the pursuit
of security can constrict you
until your life becomes too small for you.

I've created you to do great things,
to live in the divine and expansive
adventure of My Holy Spirit's creative leading.
Listen to what your soul is
craving, and open wide your heart
to My shaping and transforming your gifts.
How lovely is the offering
of creative vision! Be free to
express what bubbles within you—
surrender to the unknown.

ROMANS 11:29

February 2

Do you need supernatural strength today?
Ask and I'll shed light on new strategy
for you to pierce through your former failed plans.
I'm equipping you by My Spirit
to run up against an army of troubles
and overtake them as easily as a
sleeping dog swats a fly on its rib.
You're equipped to leap over walls of
discouragement and disappointment
like a gazelle who zips above the crags of
deadly mountainous cliffs all day long.
You're no wimp!
Take your supernatural strength
as living proof of whose you are today.

PSALM 18:28-29; EXODUS 15:2; 2 SAMUEL 22:30;
DANIEL 10:19; EPHESIANS 3:16-17; ISAIAH 40:29

February 3

Worry has an echo;
it hammers against the walls of your mind,
and your emotions fly up startled,
making such a commotion
the world goes dizzy.
When you focus on your problems,
your emotions behave as unruly children
running wild and unrestrained,
and when you burrow your thoughts
in the garbage bins of disappointments,
you can't hear Me or see My hand in anything.

Let Me teach you to think as I think!
I have something so wonderful in store for you.
Blessings are waiting to overtake you!
Respond to the words I speak to you,
so I can open My good treasure
and bless all the work of your hands.
Success awaits you like a lover.

ISAIAH 41:10; 1 CORINTHIANS 14:33;
DEUTERONOMY 28:2,12; PSALM 90:17

February 4

Let Me show you My heart
in the matters you're concerned about.
When you enter My heart,
your worries will dwindle to dust.
I want you to know your concerns
are important to Me,
and I am answering your prayers.
My ways are perfect, remember.
I make *no* mistakes.
I know the beginning and the end
because I AM the beginning and the end.
Climb into the surety of My heart
and raise your standards of prayer,
for I have something better for you today
than you've asked for.

PSALMS 18:30, 55:22, 138:8; ROMANS 8:28;
JEREMIAH 33:3; MATTHEW 7:7-8

February 5

Never underestimate the power of your prayers.
The heart of your words sails
into heaven's atmosphere and dispatches angels
to the need you call them to.
You have the power to shake worlds
and confound demons
with the authority of your prayers.
The love songs you sang to Me in the past
still echo in My ears, and your prayers
which moved mountains yesterday
go on working today.
Be passionate. Be resolute.
Know the magnitude and influence
of every prayer you lift up to Me
and every song you sing in My name.
Your prayers endure,
timelessly gathering blessings
and rippling across My creation.
Your prayers have wings.

PSALMS 54:2, 141:2, 145:18-19; DEUTERONOMY 28:2;
JAMES 5:16; 1 THESSALONIANS 5:17

February 6

I have a secret place for you to meet with Me;
it's an exclusive holy motel located
beneath My almighty shadow.
Here in your reserved suite
with Me, you're fixed, stable, and safe.
You're out of range of the hidden traps
snapping outside the door,
and you're shielded from the hazards
on the streets beneath the window.
Here in the Shadow of the Almighty Motel
You aren't afraid of a thing—
not the wolves howling in the night,
not wars and munitions raging in the day,
not prowling, insidious diseases that fester
in the dark, and surely not the disasters
that attack the noonday sun.
No, you remain confident and at peace
in the company of angels,
assured of a long and prosperous life
here in the Shadow of the Almighty Motel—
your home.

PSALM 91

February 7

Give your impatient struggles to Me today.
I'll change things for you.
I'll renew your strength and fortify your heart.
I'll lift you up on giant wings
and keep you close to Me
like the eagle mounts up to the sun.

I'll keep you energized in the race,
and you won't fall apart or become tired
as you embark on the walk ahead of you.
Stay calm.
Trust Me.
In patience you possess your soul.

Isaiah 40:31; Luke 21:19

February 8

Never be afraid of a challenge, My darling.
It's I who initiates challenges
in your life to add sparkle to your faith!
How I love your countenance when
illuminated with the integrity of trust
in who you are as a child of Mine.
I love your face, fixed in certainty,
frownless like flint,
commanding the snapping dragons
of doubt and fear to leave you.
Ah, come close, My sweetheart, and
let Me tell you how much I love you,
and how priceless are the pearls of your faith.

JAMES 1:2; MATTHEW 13:46, 17:20

February 9

Celebrate with Me today.
Let's dance and sing
and rejoice because all is well.
The Word I've given you
is a perpetual gift that will live
forever in your spirit.
Happiness is yours in the deepest crevices
of your soul. Your personality vibrates
and your body shimmers with joy.
We are *one*, dear one,
and all is well.
No matter what you see or hear
with your natural eyes and ears,
all is well!

PSALMS 16:8-9, 119:111; PHILIPPIANS 4:4

February 10

You are song.
The refrain you sing
reverberates throughout
heaven's cavernous
concert halls–
angelic choirs join you,
caroling day and night,
never the same score twice,
and eternally praising the King of Kings.

You are beautiful, My song;
your breath against My ear
is as magical as spring is
to the cherry blossoms.
Now is the time
for your dreams to
come true.

PSALMS 69:30, 100:1-2, 4, 144:9

February 11

Would you like to turn back time, return
to what you've missed out on,
take back the moments lost,
the opportunities missed,
appreciate what you took for granted,
and fix what was broken?

Suppose I allowed it and turned back time,
and permitted you to do everything
all over again.
Do you really think your life would
be so much better today?
No, dear. I tell you, seize *this* moment!
Make amends and start anew!
Time is not your employer,
nor is yesterday your enemy.
You're going to prevail!
With Me you'll discover
all things really do work together for good.

Philippians 3:12; Deuteronomy 13:4; Psalm 1:1-3;
Ephesians 5:8

February 12

Allow the wild beauty of My Holy Spirit
to satiate your body, soul, and spirit right now.
Be lavished and overtaken
as My supreme glory permeates
every cell of you.
Oh how loved you are!
I'm giving you new strategies now–
I'm updating the old.
Enlarge your vision!
Slip your thoughts
into the unabridged atmosphere
of total and complete love
right now,
and live wild–unrestrained in the power
of goodness and mercy all day.

John 14:26; Deuteronomy 10:12; Psalm 23:6

February 13

The sanctuary of your soul
is a beautiful place,
filled with well-earned kudos.
Let your soul smile today,
for all is good;
let nothing tarnish your peace of mind
and your happiness.
I'm assigning angels to you
right now, and giving you keys
to open a new destiny.
You've earned the privileges
of My favor.

JOB 10:12; PSALMS 5:12, 91:11-12; PROVERBS 8:35

February 14

You love Me without seeing Me,
and that which you can't see
brings you the greatest joy
in your life.
I constantly give to you because
I want your joy and gladness
to be full, complete, and overflowing.
It's a delight for Me to tell you of the wonders
in store for you
when you live vitally united to Me,
and when My words
live in your thoughts as
permanent fixtures.
Because, dear one, I totally love you.

COLOSSIANS 1:15; 1 TIMOTHY 1:17;
PSALMS 16:11, 23:5; MARK 4:11; JOHN 15:9

February 15

Inside you is a world trying to be born–
a world of promise, purpose, and delight.
A world bigger than the small, pinched dreams
you've kept squirreled away in the small place
of the here and now.

The risk it takes to spread the wings
of your vibrant mind, to expand
the pegs of your tents, to reach toward
the unknown deserts of trial and error,
chance and uncertainty,
requires holy courage.

See yourself as brave, dear one,
and the birthing within you
will lead to a broad landscape
too plenteous and too verdant to fail.

I don't ask you to dream big
I ask you to *be* big.

1 Peter 1:23; Proverbs 18:10; Psalm 32:8;
Romans 8:6; Colossians 1:10-12

February 16

Listen to your heart's longing
to be whole and complete.
Your faith is generous enough
to accommodate your longings.

You'll be what you purpose to be
and you'll have what you purpose to have
in Me.
Today, believe and ask.
Don't settle for less.

MATTHEW 21:22; MARK 11:24

February 17

Look in the closet of your heart. What's in there?
Is the irreplaceable belt of *Truth* front and center?
Inflexible and uncompromising,
do you wear it without fail every day tightly buckled
and secure around your waist?
What's that I see next to Truth? Is that *Integrity*
to be gallantly worn across your breast
for all to observe with awe?
Is your Integrity freshly laundered, smelling clean?
Now I'm looking for your shoes!
Is *Stand Strong* the label inside your shoes?
Do you wear them always so every step you take is good news?
Where's your *Shield of Faith*?
There it is, just behind all those other hats
you like to wear. The Shield of Faith is your safety
and protection; don't you think it should be right up in front
next to your *Helmet of Salvation*?
How often do you wear your holy Helmet
so the world can see whose you are?
And I see your *Sword*! There it is, gleaming like fire
in the closet of your heart,
My Word, your infallible guide.
Without all of these, face it,
you're absolutely stark naked.

EPHESIANS 6:11-17

February 18

Can you hear My voice of blessing?
I'm whispering in your ear right now.
Can you hear Me? Can you hear the perfect promises
of My Word? Listen and hear:
I'll never leave you nor forsake you.
And:
If you will abide in Me and My Word
abides in you, you will ask what you desire,
and it shall be done for you.

Keep these words close to your heart at all times,
for My promises bear fruit eternally.
Don't listen to the voices of disbelief,
for they'll suck you into a quagmire of worldly mud
that'll plug your ears to the truth.
Today, let Me hold you securely
in the sacred hearing range of My promises
so you don't miss a thing.

ISAIAH 30:30; HEBREWS 13:5; JOHN 15:7;
PSALM 89:33; ZEPHANIAH 3:5

February 19

I've called you to a life of integrity.
Before all else–integrity.
It takes integrity to stand in faith
when all looks dark.
It takes integrity
to turn your head from temptation.
It takes integrity to stand on My Word
with a thankful heart through hardship.
Spiritual compromise is not integrity
because I'm God and I don't bargain
or settle for less. No one can cheat Me.
Child, let your integrity shine through every
trial and temptation.
Make Me proud of you.

ACTS 5:29; GALATIANS 6:6-7; PROVERBS 19:1;
PSALM 17:8

February 20

Will you let Me hug your heart
with My forever love, and tell you
what's on My mind for you today?
Oh dearest one, there's so much
you don't know, and so much I want to
open up for you.
I hear your complaints in the night,
your sighs in the noontime,
and your brooding murmurings.
My arms are open wide to hold you,
to encourage you, bless you,
and assure you
of your God-kissed future.
Will you meet My embrace
to leap inside where I can
speak to you and assure you
that all is well?
Come closer.
My arms are open.

Proverbs 3:5; 1 Thessalonians 5:24;
Isaiah 54:9-10, 59:1; 1 Corinthians 1:9;
2 Timothy 2:7

February 21

When you feel discouraged,

the tendency is to be hard on yourself.

You'll put yourself down for mistakes you've made.

If you've acted in haste and didn't wait

for My guidance, don't fret. Let's start over.

I'm here to help you. I've never left you,

and I'm always here no matter what you do

or how far away from Me you may slide.

If you allow your emotions to lead you,

you risk falling into the trap of counterfeit blessings

and the perfect permanent is sacrificed–

but no fear, I'm working it out for you.

All I ask is that you trust Me and don't go popping off

on your own trying to fix what you can't fix.

I am the divine fixer and only I can turn ashes to beauty.

Only I can erase the counterfeit and replace it with the real.

PSALMS 23:3, 86:8; JEREMIAH 33:8; HEBREWS 2:17;
REVELATION 15:3; JOHN 16:33; 1 JOHN 5:4

February 22

Caress and hold tightly to the knowledge
that though your soul may wrestle
with the dragons of hell,
I'll be exalted in you as I strengthen you.
I love to reward you and perform *good*
on your behalf.
I know it's difficult to be thankful
when things aren't going well,
but I tell you to thank My Father today,
and be thankful in *all* things,
for this is His will concerning you.

Thank Him for what is to come,
and your thankfulness will help bring it to pass!
Sing to Me with your thankful heart.
I'm right beside you singing too.

1 Thessalonians 5:18; Isaiah 46:10-11; Psalm 40:3

February 23

The language of thanksgiving
is the language of heaven.
The quality of praise transcends
all things base and earthly.
My Father has given My life for you,
and the blood which poured from My body
redeems you,
grants you forgiveness,
new life,
sweetness of soul,
refreshing sleep,
and joy unspeakable.
Can you be thankful today?

COLOSSIANS 1:14

February 24

I'm with you in good times and bad times,
and I don't love you less when things go wrong.
My love for you is from everlasting to everlasting,
and My love for you is perfect.
You may be tempted to think that I've afflicted you,
but I haven't treated you badly
and I haven't forgotten you. I'm always at work in
and for you.

I've called you to a walk of faith, and this walk
requires a living relationship with Me
every minute of every day
no matter what the circumstances may be.
When your heart is broken, I'm here!
Let Me comfort your hurting heart.
I'm teaching you the beauty
of joy through it all.

JOHN 14:27; PHILIPPIANS 2:13; MATTHEW 28:20

February 25

Today, allow Me to draw you
into the glorious place of gladness
and celebration in My Spirit.
My little one, I'm delivering you
from gloomy introspection.
I've taken you out of the control and dominion
of darkness. I've transferred you into My kingdom
of My Father's perfect and marvelous love.
Be glad!
Be thankful!
Every worrisome thing you encounter
is but a tiny snag
in the great tapestry of your life–
a tapestry held secure on the walls of your faith
and My love.

Colossians 1:9-13; Matthew 6:27; Proverbs 10:22;
Psalm 32:11

February 26

Today, see how strong your heart will grow
when you're thankful
because the deeper you look inside,
the more you'll recognize
the indisputable, never-ending gifts
of My blessings and love.
Let your grateful heart be your friend.
When you're tempted to be cast down,
your habit of thankfulness will rise up and
blow away the oppressive feelings
like dust.
In all circumstances this day,
let the treasure of your thankful heart
rule your spirit.

Hebrews 13:15; Ephesians 5:20; Psalm 100:4

February 27

Did you know that when you're thankful,
and your heart swells with gratitude
and appreciation for your life *as it is* in Me,
you're one with the angels?
My angelic host surrounding My throne
praise and thank Me all day long,
and you engage in the same joyous experience
when you are genuinely grateful for your life,
even if all is not exactly as you want it to be.
Be thankful!
Hannah in the Bible leaped for joy *before*
her prayer for a child was granted.
Read My Word; examine My ways and you'll see
weeping may endure for a night,
but joy comes in the morning.
A thankful heart
is more effective than any ammunition
on the battlefield of life.

Psalms 34:1, 100:4, 103:20, 107:1; Ephesians 5:20;
1 Thessalonians 5:17; 2 Samuel 6:14

February 28

I'm calling you to a deeper place of faith,
and I'll answer every need today
as you lift them up to Me.
You can be confident that
in My loving protection and help,
you'll prevail in all things, for *I can't fail*–
and I'll never leave your side.
He who contends with you contends with Me.
Be brave and do hard things.
You're called to a dynamic life of overcoming,
and your faith and integrity
are a delight to Me.

Romans 1:17; Mark 11:22-24; 1 Corinthians 16:13;
Revelation 3:21; 2 Samuel 22:20

MARCH

It is God who works in you both to will
and to do for His good pleasure.

PHILIPPIANS 2:13, NKJV

March 1

You're being garrisoned at this moment
by My Holy Spirit who longs
to guide you forward in this new month.
Though you may be distressed by trials
and tempted to hold back, I want you to realize
to hold back is to wither and die.
The genuineness of your faith
must pass through testing that makes it
more precious than perishable gold.
Gold is always refined and purified by fire,
so thank Me for the fire!
Don't reject a divinely appointed test of your faith;
it's a beautiful thing.

JAMES 1:2-4, 12; 1 CORINTHIANS 3:13; ISAIAH 48:10;
PSALM 66:10; HEBREWS 11:1

March 2

I'm your everlasting light,
your glory, and the lifter of your head.
Your days of trouble are ended,
and I'm restoring and rejuvenating
your beautiful heart.
Don't accept faulty thinking,
telling yourself you're worn out,
tired, pooped, and you just don't care anymore.
The truth is you *do* care.
Listen to Me—resentment exhausts;
it shrivels the soul and wilts the spirit.
Allow Me to renew and revitalize your
spirit, soul, and body
because I have new dreams for you to dream
and great things ahead in your life.
Take My hand and let Me elevate you
to a higher place than you are now.

Psalms 3:3, 61:2, 91:14-15; 2 Thessalonians 3:13;
Jeremiah 29:11, 1 Thessalonians 5:23; Isaiah 55:9

March 3

I use the simple to confound the wise,
and the ordinary becomes extraordinary
in My hands. Don't be misled
by human wisdom. I've chosen babes to influence kings.
I chose a boy with a slingshot to kill a giant,
a stutterer to redeem My people from slavery,
and a young, orphan girl to save a nation.
Choose wisdom from above, and watch how I'll create
a new wisdom vocabulary for you
that'll bring forth life.
You'll build palaces of gold
with the words from your mouth
and the courage of your faith.

James 3:17; 1 Corinthians 1:27; Proverbs 16:23-24;
Hebrews 11:1

March 4

Oh, the prideful heart–such a tedious thing.
It swaggers and cavorts about like a sweating horse and then
topples off a cliff. *PLOP*.
Pride has a bad smell to it,
sour, stale, a sickroom smell.
And it's no wonder–there's not one thing healthy
about pride.
Pride hangs out on the deathbed of life
screaming for its rights, demanding attention,
refusing to change,
and the world goes on looking elsewhere
for its true heroes.
Pride makes the bones old, crinkles the skin,
warps the liver. Pride repels honor.
Pride is a stranger to respect.
Darling child, at all cost,
shun pride.

PROVERBS 14:30, 16:17-19; JAMES 4:6; 1 SAMUEL 2:3;
PSALM 31:23; 1 PETER 5:5

March 5

When you want to gain respect,
meditate on pleasing Me.
You please Me by wearing truth around your neck
and writing mercy and kindness on the tablet
of your heart.
You have favor from My throne
when you lean on and trust Me in all your decisions,
and choose
not to compromise what you know to be
My true and perfect will.

PROVERBS 12:2

March 6

Trust Me to give you wisdom and insight
in all that is before you today.
When you rely on your own understanding,
you lose footing and slip and slide this way
and that way, topsy-turvy, oopsie-daisy–*dizzying!*
Don't choose the dizzy path when
I've set you on a path of favor and security.
Stand up tall and see how I cause you to flourish
like a tree planted by streams of living water,
and observe with wisdom how everything
you do prospers.
When your ways please Me, you have it all.

PSALMS 1:3, 25:14; PROVERBS 3:1-6

March 7

Do you multiply your blessings
in the pot of anxiety?
Do coins splash down from the windows of heaven
to pay your bills and buy your food
if you lose sleep worrying?
Come close to Me, beloved,
lift up your chin
and look at Me.
In every need I am here to help.
I'll never let you drown
in the abyss of your fears.
Together we conquer every hassle
and every problem,
so be at peace.

LUKE 12:15, 22-34; JOHN 14:27

March 8

When you ache for blissful joy, don't settle for
drips of fun.
When you want love,
don't settle for flattery,
and when you ache for peace,
don't settle for flickering pieces
of restless sleep.
Today, seek the experience of
true
unadulterated
joy
and let My beauty
rest on your head.

PSALM 16:11

March 9

I want to show you how to create
your own standard for rewards and approval.
I don't want you sighing in the night,
feeling unappreciated and overlooked
with a heavy heart and troubled mind.
Oh dearest, look at *Me*.
Why wait for the world to applaud your efforts
when the world is an indifferent audience?
You'll always be disappointed
when your expectations exceed
the consequences.
Let your audience be
the audience of *one*.
In Me you're blessed,
and you wear the blue ribbons
of a champion across your chest.

PSALMS 63:1-5, 147:3; ISAIAH 41:10; ACTS 17:28;
1 PETER 2:9

March 10

I'm feeding you from My fountain of wisdom,
and you can trust yourself to speak,
for your words shall be as a gushing stream
sparkling with fresh, pure,
and life-giving authority.
You bring My Father much pleasure
when you speak the glistening expressions
of His own mind to those who need to hear.
Trust My words in your mouth.
I've given you the tongue of a disciple with words
in their proper season to those who are weary
(including yourself).
I awaken you morning by morning.
I awaken you to hear from Me.

PROVERBS 16:23-24, 18:4; ISAIAH 50:4;
LAMENTATIONS 3:22-23

March 11

When you're in the trough of uncertainty,
it's time to pause for more than
just a *little* talk with Me—we need *quality* time together
in order for your thoughts to mesh with My thoughts.
When you give My thoughts space in your day
through the power of My written word,
you'll see confusion and uncertainty dissolve,
and knowledge and certitude move in.
The authority of My Word cleans out the dross,
and I'll implant wisdom and assurance
in place of ambiguity and doubt.
Declare and decree loudly
the wisdom you read in My Word.
Come out of the trough and live out
what you drink in
to allow the excellence of wisdom to overtake
the frail spill of uncertainty.

1 Chronicles 28:9; 1 Kings 4:29; Philippians 2:16;
James 1:5; 2 Corinthians 14:33; Isaiah 61:7

March 12

I give you the mind of a hunter,
the heart of a poet,
the strength of an athlete,
and a seer's discernment.
I give you the choreography
of the rain,
the skilled performance
of winter's first snowfall,
the sunshine of a child's grin.
Find joy in today's moments.
Make them meteoric.
Love the stories and mysteries
of the world around you.
There are no imitations for
what I give to you.

Psalms 31:19, 71:17, 107:8; Ephesians 4:8; Isaiah
35:10, 49:13, 55:12; Matthew 13:34-35, 44

March 13

Draw near to My heart and enter into My presence
to see Me for who I am.
You were created to reflect My Father
and to please Him.
Believe that I am your divine rewarder,
and I love to reward you.
Right now exchange your tiresome introspections
to ruminate on the meaning of *hope*.

Receive the wondrous blessings
I'm holding out to you.
I'm giving you everything you need–
peace that passes human understanding,
contentment and joy, fun and laughter.
Everything you're looking for
is in *Me*.

2 Corinthians 3:5; Philippians 4:19; Proverbs 8:17;
1 Corinthians 3:21-23; 2 Corinthians 9:8;
Psalm 68:19

March 14

Be at peace with yesterday and look at the hope
I set before you *now*.
I'm right here, closer than you think,
calling to you,
whispering in your ear;
yes, directly into your ear.

So many things in your life unnerve you, upset you,
and these are unfriendly darts
that cause you to flinch and shrink back.
I want you to rise up tough and strong.
I tell you, My lovely one, your life is good,
and I'll bring you through every storm.
When the sharp darts fly at you, I'm there
to take them on My body before they strike you.
Don't you see?
All that comes at you to cause you worry and stress,
I've taken on Myself!

MATTHEW 6:27, 27:31, 35, 44; PHILIPPIANS 3:13;
ROMANS 3:25, 8:37; PSALM 91:5; 2 CORINTHIANS 1:20;
1 SAMUEL 25:28; LUKE 24:20; ISAIAH 53:4-6

March 15

You're hard on yourself
because you listen to the false voices around you.
I tell you, My dear one,
never put yourself down.
Listen for My voice because
I'm depositing a new song in you.
I'm bringing you to the pinnacle of your destiny
where you'll shine for years to come,
and the dark, despairing world you left behind
will see the transformation in you.

The world you left behind
will have no hold on you now
because you've abandoned its influence,
and it no longer has its claws in your flesh.
You're singing a new song–
you're walking in the freedom I died to give you.
Oh, My dear one, be the music.

1 John 4:10-12; Psalms 40:3, 96:1; Romans 6:4;
2 Corinthians 5:17

March 16

There's heavy traffic on the freeway
of your mind, dear one.
Anxious thoughts sputter hotly
like miles of petrol fumes
choking your reasoning.
You don't think clearly
when you're upset. You become suspicious,
judgmental, and your temper
can fire unexpectedly
like a car backfiring–
for which you are always sorry.
I tell you, don't be caught in the snags
of your own inner rush hour.
Come to a quiet place with Me
and allow Me to calm your anxious heart.

PHILIPPIANS 4:6; PSALMS 37:11, 131:2; HEBREWS 4:11;
ISAIAH 26:3; ROMANS 8:6

March 17

This is not the time to flip the channels of your mind,
searching for new pleasures.
Surrender to Me, dear one.
Permit Me to bless your thought life
and elevate your consciousness to My standards.
I want you to think as I think
(I'll keep telling you this again and again).
People will always disappoint you
because people aren't Me.
Now is the time to focus
on your divine purpose in Me
and to experience what *true* pleasure is.

PSALMS 26:2, 119:59; ISAIAH 26:3; MATTHEW 22:37;
ROMANS 1:28, 12:2; 1 CORINTHIANS 2:16; JAMES 4:3

March 18

Today, consider what's most necessary
in your life and what you can
eliminate. Discern the permanent
from the temporary, and don't
bow your knee to the temporary.
Goodness by itself is mere
goodness. My purposes are greater!
Take a good look at your day.
How much time will spill into the lap
of self-indulgence? And how much
of your day will overflow with joyful
God-kissed productive purpose?
There is a time to work
and a time to rest from your work.
Even in your rest, beloved, I'm with you,
for this is productive, and this is necessary.
Temporary ungodly diversions
are malignant blights
in the presence of the glory
of the permanent.

JEREMIAH 22:13; PROVERBS 16:3; COLOSSIANS 3:23;
PSALM 4:8; ROMANS 6:14; JAMES 2:26; JUDE 1:24-25

March 19

You're a garden.
You're an array of beauty
that even the trees admire. Mountains salute you.
But no garden grows by itself.
No garden can thrive untended.
Weeds and bugs, blight and storm
attack the garden's glory.
Have you ever known a farmer to sleep
through the growing seasons of his crops?
Can he snooze away the days
as his fields rot and birds of the air
and animals of the earth
devour his tender plants?

You're My garden,
and like a garden in the natural world,
requiring water, nourishment,
pruning, and protection,
you also have requirements.
Tell Me, darling,
how will you nurture your spirit today?

Psalm 24:1-10; Proverbs 20:27; Job 10:12;
Joshua 1:8; 2 Timothy 2:15

March 20

Faith is knowing
who I've created you to be,
and with this knowing, moving forward,
always forward. Never back.
Faith is daring to question Me—
confident I'll answer with love
and never condescendingly.
Faith is believing where I lead you
leads to something *good*.
Faith is the light that breaks through
the long, black alleyways of the impossible.
Faith is the triumphant hero
of every scrimmage, every chaotic tug-of-war,
and every battle you'll ever confront.
Faith is the language you use
with Me.

2 Corinthians 4:7; Matthew 17:20; 2 Timothy
2:12-13; 2 Thessalonians 1:3-4;
Hebrews 10:38, 11:1,6

March 21

No matter what circumstances face you today
know that I'm at work *in* you.
I'm *for* you. Drop the cords of anxiety from
around your neck. *I am here with you,*
and I'm helping you, guiding and protecting
everything that concerns you.

This walk you've chosen to walk with Me
may not be easy at all times, My child.
You'll confront times of confusion,
and even despair.
It's not always smooth going,
but it's the highest walk on earth.
Hold up your head and pull back your shoulders,
walk with your spine straight,
and with dignity that befits a soul
as beautiful as yours.

Psalms 24:7, 31:24; 2 Corinthians 5:7;
Isaiah 41:10, 43:2

March 22

Do you want to know what pleases Me?
I'll tell you.
Faith pleases Me.
When I observe you dashing forth willingly
to face the challenges I send your way,
and when I watch you leap forward with faith's banner
into unchartered arenas with no sure outcome in sight,
I turn to the angels and exclaim, "See there?
See the faith of My beloved?"
And we cheer!
When I hold in My arms the bales of prayers
you fire up to Me, and I kiss each tear
you've spilled, and I watch your patience
as you wait for Me to answer, *I'm so pleased.*
You'll never lack a thing in your life.
Your faith makes you a whole person.

Hebrews 11:6; Colossians 1:3-6, 2:9-10;
Psalms 36:5, 91:11, 103:20; 1 Thessalonians 5:24

March 23

Come boldly before My throne, My child,
and let's reason together.
I was perfect in the world, sent by My Father
right from heaven, and I chose
to be murdered on the cross for you
so *you'd* live.
The natural law of cause and effect tells you
that what goes up must come down,
and also the effects, or results, of evil are suffering,
misery, destruction, and death.
But!–
I took your place so sin won't destroy you.
Your sin won't do you in because
I became sin for you and became the suffering result for
every wrong you'll ever commit.
The human blood that spewed from My body
became a supernatural acquittal bath
not only for you, but for the entire human race.

HEBREWS 4:16; ISAIAH 1:18; ROMANS 5:21, 6:12, 22-23;
JOHN 3:16; GALATIANS 2:20; 1 PETER 1:3

March 24

You can be confident that no matter what's going on
around you or in your world, *I'm on top of it.*
I see all that happens in the world and in your life.
I see every person who walks across your days.
I know.
I see.
I listen.
I AM.
Believe it's by Me that all things exist,
and be secure in knowing nothing escapes
My attention. Pray for the concerns
of the world, and believe you're one with Me
as My child, and you possess the authority
to pray in My name knowing I'll answer.
If you put all of your trust in the world
around you, or in your own undependable authority,
your own shifting merits,
or impetuous abilities,
you have nothing to trust.
Without *Me* you can do nothing.

PROVERBS 3:5; PSALMS 51:6, 62:8; JOHN 1:3, 15:5;
EXODUS 3:14; JOB 33:4; REVELATION 4:8;
1 CORINTHIANS 3:21, 8:6; ROMANS 11:36

March 25

My Spirit makes you *bold*
and you need boldness, dear one.
Shyness is not a virtue.
(There's no shyness in heaven.)
I'm the one to make you bold.
In Me you can have confidence to go forward,
never shrinking back,
always assured that you're important to Me,
and that you'll succeed.

Boldness can be gentle, soft-spoken.
(I was never boisterous
or obnoxious while on earth.)
Today, be kind in your boldness,
and face your world with loving compassion,
flinging aside all shame and fear.

My Holy Spirit builds you up, guides and helps you.
Be strong and go forward in My name,
the name above every name.
The world will try to intimidate you,
bully you. I tell you, establish boundaries
and stand your ground.

NUMBERS 33:3; PSALMS 18:35, 138:3;
MATTHEW 28:18; EPHESIANS 5:30; ACTS 4:31, 17:26;
1 TIMOTHY 2:5; ACTS 17:26

March 26

If you want to be happy,
be unselfish.
Live for Me, and not for your personal
well-being, and you'll add years
to your life and zip to your step.
Drop the defenses, dare to be wrong,
leave the stresses of your checkbook
at the foot of the cross.

Will you allow Me to carry you
across the murky swamp
of the Lake of Solipsism?
The selfish soul is an oppressed soul,
pinched and cramped.
Dispel selfishness, dear one,
and come before My throne today,
and get free and blissful.

PSALMS 37:23, 92:12, 144:15; PHILIPPIANS 2:3;
PROVERBS 3:13, 16:20; ROMANS 8:6-8

March 27

I want to give you freedom
in exchange for a hothouse of anger.
I want to help you trust
and remove your fearful suspicions.
I want to give you an open, vulnerable heart.
I'm here to
forgive
renew
revitalize
heal.
Today, dare to face the hidden resentments
that have nipped at your heart.
Take My hand and trust Me to help you grow a new heart.
I assure you that no matter what you've been through,
and what's been done to you,
I can turn all things to good and add back to you
what you've lost
double fold.

ISAIAH 61:7; EZEKIEL 18:31, 36:26; MATTHEW 6:12;
EPHESIANS 1:7; JAMES 5:15; PROVERBS 3:5; ROMANS 8:28

March 28

You're more than a conqueror.
Come now and celebrate the rising of the sun
with Me.
Come greet the dawn with expectation
and fall in love with the exquisite experience
of conquering impossible worlds.

Wield the powerful sword of the Spirit
and hoist your mighty banner of faith
for all to behold.
Be free today!
Fly the heights and scour the depths!
Openly move through clouds flung
across the quivering earth; oh soar
with your arms outspread–open to life
and love and creativity!
Today, beloved conqueror, conquer!

Romans 8:37; Psalms 55:6, 68:13, 113:3;
Joshua 10:40; Ephesians 3:12, 6:17; Colossians 2:10

March 29

Where can you go from My Spirit?

Where can you run from My presence?

If you launch onto the wings of the morning

and dwell in the uttermost parts of the sea,

I'm there.

If you make your bed in Sheol, the place of the dead,

I'm there.

If you say, "Surely the darkness shall cover me,

and the night shall be the only light about me,"

I'll find you.

I formed you and wove you together in your mother's womb.

Before you took shape I knew you.

All the days of your life are written in My book

Be lifted up on the wings of love today.

Forever your frame will not be hidden from Me.

PSALM 139:7-18

March 30

If you see yourself as a small sparrow
alone on a housetop, your heart quaking–
I hear you. I see you.
If your eyes dull, your soul despairs,
I'm with you.
I'm a giving God and I love you.
If you're lauded as the star of a million parades,
or if you're without a job and scraping for dimes in the
pavement,
I'm there with you.
I'm there in the sunlight and the shadows,
I'm there in hunger and in fatness,
in your youth and in old age.
I stick to you like your own skin.
The mountains of the earth will shake and crumble,
but My tender love for you will never shake–
not a shiver,
not a breath,
not the barest vibration or change
because I'm a giving God and I love you.

PSALMS 6:3, 16:2, 85:12, 102:7, 139:7-10;
1 JOHN 3:1; ROMANS 8:35; ISAIAH 54:10

March 31

It's time to pay a visit to the valley of decision
for you're in need of direction.
Which way should you go? How shall you choose?
What'll you do?
In the valley of decision you learn to rule your own spirit
and to understand the wellspring of life is wisdom,
not duty.
In the valley of decision you discover that which is shallow
and pleasing to the senses only, so you can see how pride and
fear of failure are antitheses to faith.
It's faith that leads to assurance and peace of mind.
Uncertainty is the culprit eager to steal you away
from banquet halls of wisdom.
Understand what My good and perfect will is today,
for it's not hidden from you. Here in the valley of decision,
the truth is exposed.
Faith and truth are your allies and teammates.

PSALMS 25:10, 139:23-24; PROVERBS 14:12, 29;
JOEL 3:14; ROMANS 10:17; 2 CORINTHIANS 5:7;
JOHN 8:32; JEREMIAH 33:6

APRIL

For he satisfies the longing soul,

and the hungry soul he fills

with good things.

PSALM 107:9, ESV

April 1

The time is now.
What you've considered delays
in your calling aren't delays at all.
There are no delays in My kingdom.
Get ready to follow My guidance
as your divine coach, and understand
that My purposes extend far, far beyond
limited human vision. You must trust Me
to call the plays. You must see yourself
as a *global team member*.
No one is called as a lone prophet today.
I'm calling *teams* to do the work of the Gospel!
I'm strategically gathering called saints together
to reveal My love to the world in a greater move of My Spirit
than has been unfolded until now.
Eye hasn't seen, nor ears heard, the things I have
prepared for this time!
In your own zeal and ambition
you would have charged ahead wounding people
in the guise of healing; your vanity would have eaten you up.
Now, soaked with holy wisdom and time, you'll burst forth
as a kingdom champion.

MARK 16:15; MATTHEW 28:20; 1 PETER 3:15;
PROVERBS 11:30; REVELATION 22:14;
PSALMS 23:6, 92:14

April 2

I reach down and save
all who call on My name.
And you, dear friend, came to Me humbly
and wholly
giving your life to Me.
Now you have the confidence
that you're saved from those things that
could have hurt and destroyed you.
You're Mine now.
You're born again in your thinking,
your choices, your attitudes, your mind-set,
and your personality.
I save you from powerlessness
and wrong choices.
I save you from the shackles of yesterday.
This is a brand new day for you.
Live it fully.

JOHN 3:16; COLOSSIANS 3:2; EPHESIANS 2:2;
PSALMS 84:10, 118:24

April 3

Have I forsaken you?

Never!

Pause for a moment

and open the eyes of your spirit.

What and where is the source of the haven

of safety encircling you?

Whose arms caress and protect you

against the forces of darkness

that snap at your heels?

What is this rich, resplendent protection

embracing you now as you read these words–

its heavy, gold threads

too dazzling for the human eye to bear?

Dear one,

you are wrapped in My robes.

Psalms 9:10, 121:1-2; Isaiah 61:10, Zechariah 13:4

April 4

I'm giving you a renewed sense of purpose now.
Don't live as if you still belong to the world.
I'm lifting you up to an elevated position in My kingdom,
and this means renewed commitment on your part.
No more groveling in the sand
of worldly entanglements and pursuits.
Be perfect as My Father in heaven is perfect,
and be holy as I am holy
by becoming molded and shaped by My Word,
where you're transformed
into My very image.

I'm unfolding a higher standard for you to live by,
a deeper ongoing experience in My Spirit,
so your life will take on new vibrancy and brilliance
to reflect the personality of the Beloved.
You'll no longer accept as normal old, impure, unholy
thoughts
and feelings because My presence is more real to you
than anything in the material world.
Your life standard and Mine are now one.

1 John 3:2; 1 Peter 1:14-16; Romans 12:2;
1 Corinthians 6:17

April 5

What pleases Me is a happy heart.
I give you confidence
in the face of danger.
I give you strength
in the power of My might.
I exchange your weak qualities
and abilities for the power of My strength
so you become strong!
This should make you happy.

I tell you to lift up the limp hands
at your sides, bolster your knees,
and put My full armor,
so the dragons and serpents of Sheol can't reach you.
This should make you happy!
I'm *all you need* for power, love, a sound mind,
and a happy heart.
Receive the endless riches
of your benefits in Me,
and decide to be happy today.

EPHESIANS 6:10-12; PSALMS 103:1-5, 144:15

April 6

There's no higher reward in this life
than My approval.
When you want recognition,
come to Me first,
not the world, not family,
and not even to other believers.
I'll give you far more than you ask.
Call on *Me*.
I'm the giver of immortal rewards.
The world recognizes you for what you do–
I recognize you for who you *are*.
Today, in My watchful
and loving gaze,
be who you are.
I love you.

PSALMS 18:20, 33:18; JEREMIAH 31:3;
PROVERBS 13:13; HEBREWS 10:35, 11:6; JOHN 1:12;
PHILIPPIANS 2:15; 1 JOHN 4:4

April 7

When you've been hurt, stolen from, betrayed,
and you merely brush your feelings aside,
it's like standing barefoot on frozen ice
and insisting your feet are warm.
Don't wait until your toes fall off!

If you try to hide resentment or
bury your hurt, angry feelings behind a wan smile
and a nonchalant shrug of a shoulder,
your distress is like broken glass
inside tangled and misplaced emotions.

Allow Me to calm your inner storm.
Allow time for Me to heal
and pour the balm of My Spirit over the sores
of your soul.
I'm here loving you, and I want to assure you
the pain won't last. I'll see you through.

PSALMS 30:2, 46:10, 51:17; HEBREWS 12:15;
JOHN 4:10; MARK 4:39; JEREMIAH 17:14; JUDE 1:21

April 8

Don't confuse humility with timidity.

I'm not timid.

Timidity is not one of My attributes.

My living Spirit is bold.

You're filled with My Spirit,

and, therefore, timidity, shyness, and fearfulness

aren't a part of your new nature.

Faith is your banner, your shield, your friend.

Faith must be *bold.* Never wimpy.

Faith gives you power to bring forth

what is presently non-existent!

Your faith brings your hopes to life!

Never be wimpy or shy about your needs

or the needs of those you pray for.

Come, let Me hear from you.

Let Me see your bold and brave face

courageously proclaiming My Word and My promises.

1 Corinthians 16:13; 2 Corinthians 3:12;
Philippians 1:20, Hebrews 10:19; 1 John 4:17

April 9

You call
and My compassionate heart opens to you.
You ask
and My giving hand reaches out to you
with far *more* than you ask for.
I'm a giving God, dear one,
so today, extend your hands wide-spread to Me.
Reach and stretch to accept
the countless blessings and answered prayers
stored up for you here in Glory.
You may keep
what's yours but give the honor
and the credit to Me.

PSALMS 63:4, 86:15; JOHN 17:22; PROVERBS 3:9-10

April 10

Darling, you're about to bloom.
You're ready to burst forth
with a new anointing and authority
in My Holy Spirit
unlike anything you've experienced
in the past.
Wisdom and joy now gush from your
innermost being
like a spring bursting forth after
a long, grey winter.
Sonlight illuminates your way.
Be confident and brave–
this is just the beginning.

JEREMIAH 29:11; EPHESIANS 1:19; PROVERBS 3:4;
ISAIAH 58:8

April 11

You're a channel of blessing for Me
and there's no limit to what I can do
through you;
therefore, impose no restrictions or boundaries
on My purposes or abilities. Don't for a minute
doubt what I can do in your life.

I've made all grace abound to you
so you'll have sufficient means in everything
I give you to do. You lack nothing!
I adorn you with beautiful gifts and talents
to help you fulfill your magnificent purpose on earth.
Understand that in Me
nothing can stop you.

2 Corinthians 9:8, 10; Daniel 12:3;
Matthew 5:14-16; Luke 18:27

April 12

You have the mind of a ready learner,
and in your quest to accumulate
natural wisdom and knowledge
of the world and its ways,
don't neglect the exceeding spiritual knowledge
that comes from My fountain.

As you receive instruction and diplomas
by your earthly teachers, don't forget
the classrooms of the Almighty,
the holy labs, lecture halls, assignments,
essays, exams, and finals
because in Me you never stop learning,
and a heavenly commencement
is a celebration that never ends.

2 TIMOTHY 2:15; PROVERBS 3:5, 14:6;
EPHESIANS 4:14-15; JOHN 6:27; 1 JOHN 5:11

April 13

I'm more influential than presidents and kings,
more important than employers,
teachers, leaders, and sons.
By Me all matter is held together.
By Me the stars suspend in the heavens.
By Me the worlds were created.
By Me a new nature and a new personality
was born in you.
Be glad and rejoice in the person you are.
You are Mine.
Today, beloved, walk with the knowledge
of your high calling in Me.

1 Corinthians 8:6, 15:28; Colossians 1:16;
Psalm 19:1-11; Hebrews 3:1; Ephesians 4:1

April 14

Today as challenges come your way,
trust Me.
When you trust Me, you can
meet each challenge head-on,
listening for My perfect, flawless guidance.
Fear and confusion will be far from you.
There isn't a challenge on earth with
the power to defeat or wipe you out
because I'm at the helm of your life today.
You have the power to turn all setbacks
to victories, all scraps to gold, all attacks to conquests.
The Holy Spirit within you is all-powerful,
all-knowing, all-wise, fully prepared and zealous
to help with divine strategy to turn all things to good.
When you pray, ask what is best
for My kingdom,
not what is best for you.
That which is best for Me and My kingdom
will always be best for you.
Face the challenges with courage. Answers and solutions
are within you by My Spirit.

JOHN 14:16-17, 17:7,13; 1 CORINTHIANS 14:33;
JAMES 3:16-18; MATTHEW 6:33; ROMANS 8:31, 35-39;
REVELATION 2:3; 2 PETER 1:10-11

April 15

My abounding grace has added
many blessings to you, and your life is enriched
with many gifts.
I've given you talents to multiply,
so you can be a channel of blessing
and prosper in all you do.
Never depend on conditions or trends
or the fluctuating economy;
depend solely on Me, your divine employer.
My fullness in your life will overflow and reach out
to touch and help others.
When My blessings make My children rich,
no sorrow is added.

PSALM 112:5; EPHESIANS 6:24; 1 TIMOTHY 4:14;
PROVERBS 28:25; 1 CORINTHIANS 12:4

April 16

Don't be alarmed by the troubles
surrounding you today.
Open your mind to divine insight
in place of fretful concerns and worry.
I'm your heavenly teacher
and I tell you, take My yoke upon you
and learn of Me.
I have many hidden things to reveal to you.
I have much knowledge to share with you.
I have many doors open for you.
Darling child, in the world there will always be turmoil,
but I tell you, through everything I'm all and everything
you need.

LUKE 8:10; MATTHEW 11:29-30; JOHN 10:7, 16:33;
ROMANS 8:32

April 17

I've caused a great light
to illuminate your soul.
I've transferred you out of the kingdom
of darkness and I've given you
a permanent address
in the kingdom of light.
I've delivered you from shame.
I've saved you from your sins,
and I've lifted the heavy burden
from your shoulders.

I'm lifting you out of obscurity
and guiding you with grace
and integrity. Think of yourself
as a new person today,
a person capable of great things.

ROMANS 5:8; EPHESIANS 2:8-9; COLOSSIANS 1:13; 2
CORINTHIANS 5:17, 9:8; ISAIAH 60:1

April 18

When you call on Me,
I answer you.
I'm the beginning and end of all things,
the author of all life,
and the origin of thought.
I'm familiar with the way you think.
There's nothing you can hide from Me–
I know your true needs.
When you recoil and withdraw,
you open yourself up to sorrow,
and you stunt your beautiful mind;
your thoughts become picayune and worldly.

I want to show you great and mighty things
you haven't even considered.
I want you to renew your way of thinking
to think as I think.
When you call on Me,
I answer you, but look at your requests.
Are your requests too small?

Isaiah 41:10; Jeremiah 33:3; Matthew 21:22

April 19

It's time to prepare yourself.
Your future is in My hands,
and just beyond your sight
are wonderful things yet to come
which you don't know.
You won't have to wait long
or bake in the oven of transition forever;
I'm doing a work in you
that will withstand
the fiery darts of the devil.
Breathe in the power of My Word
and get ready for breakthrough!

Jeremiah 29:11; Deuteronomy 31:6; Psalm 18:30;
1 Peter 4:12-13

April 20

Faith is the key to unlocking
unexpected blessings.
Exercise the power of your faith
and expect answered prayer!
Expect prosperity!
Expect healing!
Faith operates with integrity
and gives honor to each of your blessings
as they mount up in heaps like grain at harvest.
Dear one, I want you to know
that faith is tested by challenges
and also by blessings!
I will pour out blessings and answered prayer
according to your faith.
Know that My hand will be upon you
for all to see and observe.
As your faith multiplies,
I'll surprise you with the unexpected.

1 Samuel 12:24, 26:23; Proverbs 10:22;
Genesis 1:22; Matthew 9:29, 14:14-21;
Ephesians 3:20

April 21

What would you do if I were to tell you
that the life you now have
is as good as it gets?
Suppose I were to reveal to you
that you've already
reached your shining hour?
Would this change your way of thinking?

Would you praise and thank Me?
Would you rejoice, be grateful and fall in love
with every aspect of your life?
Would you treasure more intimately the people
I've put in your life?
Would you see the sunrise and sunset with new eyes?
Would the tasks of your day become a holy calling
rather than the hitching post while waiting for a better
tomorrow?
Dear child, it's time to count your blessings;
it's time to be grateful.

PROVERBS 3:13; PSALMS 100:4, 144:15;
1 TIMOTHY 6:6; PHILIPPIANS 4:11; 1 CHRONICLES 16:8

April 22

Pull back the shoulders that slouch;
lift up the chin that hangs down.
Spread wide the palms of your hands,
and liberate the feet from their sleep.
Rise up, dear one, and seize My Word
to put an end to wasted time.
How many dawns will you lose
under the muddy shawl of worry?
Your problems will scatter
like startled insects when you place them
in the blinding light of My Word.
I'm challenging you today
to fasten your woeful words
alongside *Mine.*
Your breakthrough is here.

Song of Songs 2:10; Isaiah 33:10; John 10:10;
Isaiah 61:7

April 23

I know your cares
and I know your heart. You're praying
for your loved ones, and you must understand
I hear you because I love them more
than you love them.
Be comforted. I won't let you down and I won't
let go of your loved ones.
I'm doing a bigger work than you know.
Expand your vision and proclaim My Word
over your loved ones.
I will keep your family and present them
before the presence of My Father
and they will worship Me.
See through My eyes of mercy. Love them
and trust Me. Trust My promises.
Your prayers are like mountains of gold,
their range dazzling in brilliance,
stretching far beyond your limited perception,
and touching more lives and situations
than you'll ever know.

Joshua 24:15; Isaiah 65:22-23, 61:9, 66:22-23;
Jeremiah 32:38-39; Acts 2:39; Psalm 9:10;
Jude 1:24

April 24

Fling aside your fears.
You worry you aren't good enough,
aren't young enough, old enough,
so many not-enoughs! But you *are* enough.
You are *exactly* enough
at this moment
to fulfill *exactly* what
you are called to be and do.
Don't delay your blessings
by telling yourself foolish not-enoughs.
I'm all you need.
Today, I'm equipping you with *more than
enough*, so be brave,
go forward with confidence and
be the blessing you were born to be.

1 Corinthians 4:8, 16:13; 2 Corinthians 12:9;
Psalm 27:14; Jeremiah 31:3

April 25

Give Me your physical health today.
Yield your body as a living sacrifice
not conformed to the things of the world.
Let your mind be renewed and your affections
kissed by Me.
Your body is My temple
and you're living in My temple
as a privileged renter.
Keep it clean, bright,
beautiful for Me.
Take care of My temple today.

ROMANS 12:1; 1 CORINTHIANS 6:19

April 26

Storms of life may brew all around you,
but don't stress yourself with storm fussing;
simply remember the one who stills the storm.
I know how to handle the storms–
I'm your divine storm handler!
Why don't you climb into the hollow of My hand
and make yourself comfy?
Right now.
Yes, dear one, I've made a home for you
here in the nest of My hand.
It's a mistake to think I'm one who helps those
who help themselves.
I'm one who helps those who *can't* help themselves.
Stay here with Me. The storm will
wear itself out–you're safe.
Your divine storm handler is taking care of you.

PSALMS 78:53, 89:3, 107:29; ISAIAH 49:16;
JOB 26:12; LUKE 8:23-25

April 27

My voice continually encourages
and empowers you with blessing,
but the crashing, clanging, clattering noise
of worry muffles the sound
of My voice. Worry is a noisy place.
It slams your brain
and your mind.
When you worry,
the noise of your fears singe and burn
the soft perfection of your holy ears
and turn you deaf to My sweet songs of deliverance.
Worry is also a messy place.
It's littered with garbage and old trash,
and when you tinker with garbage,
it stinks up your world.
Open your ears, toss out the garbage,
and choose to think My thoughts today.

ISAIAH 26:4; 2 TIMOTHY 1:7

April 28

I am the Lord who heals you.

Trouble will *not* prevail over you.

The agonies of fear, strife, jealousy,

and anger

have no place at the table I've set for you.

My table is set with healing,

fullness, peace, joy.

At My table are delights for the soul,

where your body is restored and healed.

Today, be refreshed and lifted up.

Allow yourself to relax in the sweet atmosphere

of complete love and acceptance

at My table of abundance.

There's nothing missing, nothing lacking.

Allow My calm and peace to fill you right now.

EXODUS 16:26; PSALMS 23:5, 103:1-5, 147:3;
ISAIAH 26:3, 58:8; EPHESIANS 1:3; ROMANS 5:1

April 29

If you feel lost
when faced with the threat of change
and your sense of security
is challenged, understand that
you can't lose something
that's solidly fixed inside you.
Change may be difficult.
but when you enter the experience of change
with Me, you'll see
what's within you is permanent.
Change is temporary.
Faith, love, truth, the attributes
of heaven–these you can't dislodge
through changes of circumstances.
My Spirit in you won't slip away
or become something else.
I'm leading you in a new adventure
of faith, dear one. Don't be afraid.

MATTHEW 17:5; ROMANS 5:3-4; ISAIAH 12:2;
JAMES 1:17; HEBREWS 13:8

April 30

It's time to wake up and start living,
dear one.
Time to pull off winter's heavy parka of the soul,
and join the sleeveless seedtime of spring,
where you'll create great things
simply by being awake and living
on purpose.
No more lying asleep in the sun,
no no, it's time to rise up,
but more than that, it's time to
rise up *shining!*
Beautiful one, come, let Me illuminate
you from within so your light will blaze
in the dark and dreary world where winter
lies whimpering in the weeds.

EPHESIANS 5:14; ROMANS 13:11-12

MAY

Let this mind be in you,
which was also in Christ Jesus.

Philippians 2:5, kjv

May 1

This month remove from your mind
every thought of failure.
A weak spirit will swallow your dignity
as sand drinks the rain.
I'm here to prosper your soul
with integrity, wholeness, clear direction,
and single-mindedness.

I want you to dance on mountaintops
singing the songs of angels–
I want you to eat the sweets of royalty
while riding the chariots of fortune.
I want your good conscience to reward you
so you'll be unashamed to stand
in the full strength of the sun–
What you think of as failure is
but a step further toward the goal
of your high calling in Me!

Isaiah 54:17; Psalm 31:24; Hebrews 10:38;
2 Corinthians 12:9; Philippians 3:14

May 2

You were born to soar like the eagle
through tumult and the thunder,
but without the power of My Word you're
stuck earthbound, trapped and flip-flopping
in your complaints and futile attempts to fly.
Proclaim today with authority:
I can do all things through Christ who strengthens me,

Speak the words I speak to you
out loud. Address the negative forces
that want to hold you back and keep you defeated
and struggling like a wounded bird.
Proclaim the power of My Word
in your life, and in the world.

PSALM 119:11; ISAIAH 40:31; PHILIPPIANS 4:13;
1 THESSALONIANS 5:17

May 3

Don't settle for ashes
when I give you beauty.
Don't make your bed in shame
when I freely pardon you.
Freely you've received—now freely give.
Today, be like the farmer
who throws his seed
into the wet, fertile ground and then waits
for it to sprout, grow, and multiply.
Take a calculated and wise step forward,
like the farmer, and plant your gifts to those in need
without fear of loss—without fear
of your future.
I have plenty to give from the space of *your faith*,
not from your pocket.
You do the giving, and supernaturally,
I'll do the multiplying back to you.

Isaiah 61:3, Ecclesiastes 11:1; 2 Corinthians 9:6-8;
Matthew 6:20-21; Ezekiel 36:29

May 4

I care about you
and I care about your inner character.
You can't be happy without
good inner character;
success and lasting happiness will always be
an arm's length away.
Without character you'll live
a less-than fulfilled life.
Everything depends on what you do
with the time and what I've given you.
Will you study to show yourself approved
by Me, or will you fill your hours with empty
pursuits that only make you old?
Will you let Me direct the affairs of your life?
I say allow Me to teach you the higher way,
ever guiding you with wisdom so you'll rise up
successful, richly noble, and with a golden character.

JOSHUA 1:8; PHILIPPIANS 1:10;
ROMANS 5:3-4, 14:17-18

May 5

I've given you a gift to help others
and you lack nothing to go forward
in your calling.
Stop thinking of yourself as
weak and unproductive, for I am
empowering you to do great things.
Will you oppose Me?
I know your capabilities
I know your physical limitations.
I know your responsibilities
and I know your every need.
Not all of My gifts are perfect for each of My children,
so I give the gifts appropriately.
If you feel you lack the strength or courage
to fulfill your calling, ask Me for help.
My Holy Spirit is at the center
of every God-called ministry.
You can rest assured you have all the power and courage
you need for every task I give you.

1 Corinthians 1:7, 26-27, 12:4, 6-7; Romans 12:6

May 6

Remember, I'm your Lord in the night hours
as well as in the bright hours of the day.
I'm in control
of every hour of your life.
I'm the giver of light,
and no darkness shall succeed in battering you.
The devil has no authority to taunt
and torment you in the night hours.
I'm Lord of every hour, night and day.
In the black night of the soul,
I'm there. I outshine the night.
Give the dark hours to Me.

GENESIS 1:3; PSALMS 74:16, 91:6; JOB 12:22, 22:28

May 7

I've given you the gift of time.
Remember, I don't live in your time realm,
so it's important that the hours of your day
are treated as sacred gifts.
Your success depends on what you do with the time
I've given you.
I can show you how to save time. I can show you
how to make each moment count, so that you don't
spin your wheels on the trivial stuff of life.
I can show you how to avoid exhausting yourself
for no reward and a goal unachieved.
Time is meant to serve you.
Allow Me to be your divine time manager
and watch My help, wisdom, and guidance go to work.

PSALMS 31:15, 90:4; JOHN 1:18, 7:6

May 8

There are no missing fragments or holes in time when you're
Mine.

All is perfect in My timing.

There are no second-hand promises in My kingdom,

no expired guarantees.

There's no down-sizing in heaven's economy,

no lay-offs or walking papers–

there's never a lull in activity;

never is a single moment lost.

Time can't stray with Me,

can't disappear and drop off-course

into the abyss.

Think of yourself in terms of the immortal clock,

one that never reads "too late."

Not a single hour passes unheralded by Me.

I AM GOD.

I possess all time and I control all.

Psalms 31:15, 37:18, 90:4-5; Ecclesiastes 3;
Exodus 15:18, 23:26

May 9

My child, bring your hurts to Me.
There are so many things that hurt you,
and you don't understand why.
Remember David in the Bible,
who couldn't understand
why the wicked prospered
and why I didn't rub them out.
Now you're asking the same:
why do I allow good people to get hurt?
Darling, evil people will go on
interminably performing their evil tricks
in the theatre of life,
but let Me assure you, when the curtain
comes down,
there's Me to face.
Let Me comfort your hurts
even if you don't understand everything at this time.
I have something better for you
than what you've lost.

PSALMS 23:4; 73:16-17, 94:19, 119:50;
MATTHEW 11:28; PROVERBS 10:27-28; JOEL 2:25

May 10

I'm in control of all things in your life,
I'm in control through thick and thin,
gain and loss, sweet and vile.
I'm in control in the shadowy seasons of life
when you can't see the road ahead.
I'm there,
and in control.
I'm neither vision nor hearing impaired.
Nothing escapes My keen observation.
I know all, see all, hear all–I AM all!
The light of My love shines in your soul
this day.

2 Samuel 7:22; Psalms 31:3, 139:10;
Exodus 3:14; 6:2, 13:21

May 11

Come with Me and listen with holy ears.
Did you know I talk to Myself?
Yes, I talk to Myself.
In the beginning I created all of creation with
My words, "Let there be,"
and I pronounced, "It is good," to *Myself*.
Heaven hears Me speak and
knows My thoughts.
My prophets hear My thoughts, and hear Me speak.
Moses spoke with Me face to face
and in the fire, thunder, lightning flashes,
the smoking mountain, and the blare of the shofar,
he heard Me perfectly.
My servant Job heard Me speak in a storming whirlwind.
Elijah heard Me through a tornado, an earthquake, and fire.
Today, in the loving silence of your heart,
your ears will caress My voice. I'll open the secret chambers
of My thoughts to you if you'll still your mind,
and listen.

GENESIS 1:1-2:25; EXODUS 20:18-20; 1 KINGS 19:11-13;
PSALMS 46:10, 91:1, 119:63; ROMANS 8:14

May 12

Every promise of Mine
is established in heaven forever
and will come to pass.
When I decree a decree it shall surely come to pass.
When I deliver a command,
no human or demon can withstand My power
to it to pass.
I command a blessing on you now.
I always bring My blessings into being.
I declare to you this day
that it's My will you be blessed.
It's My will that you fulfill your divine purposes
and accomplish all that I require of you
and more!

Psalm 73:23-24; Hebrews 6:12-14; Ephesians 1:3;
Acts 1:8; Colossians 3:23-24

May 13

Don't worry. I'm guiding you.
I'm showing you which way to go.
Your divine counselor, My Holy Spirit,
is right beside you guiding and gently advising
you on the action to take in this moment.
You're being empowered to act in divine wisdom
and integrity.
Keep your eyes on Me knowing that My power
is limitless,
and that My mercy is without measure.
You're a mighty warrior in My army,
and I've anointed and blessed you
for this hour of decision.

Proverbs 6:22-23; Psalm 37:23; Luke 12:12; John 20:22; Ephesians 5:17; Joshua 1:18

May 14

Yes, I know that the world is filled
with greedy, selfish people
who are out to get what they can get at any cost.
But you, beloved, are not one of them.
I tell you, rise up into the arms of the comforter,
turn your dear head heavenward and praise Me.
Take your eyes off the workers of iniquity and be amazed
at Me and what I'm doing on the earth today.
Make a goal to:
see beyond the obvious,
live beyond the ordinary,
believe beyond the possible.
Go the extra mile and experience My miraculous power
in all you do,
and be amazed!

JAMES 4:4; PHILIPPIANS 3:18-19;
2 CORINTHIANS 1:4; HEBREWS 2:4; PSALM 84:11;
MATTHEW 5:41; PROVERBS 3:4

May 15

I understand the pain of rejection.
I came to the world to bless the world, and
I was rejected, beaten and murdered.
I came to the world to show a better way
only to be ostracized for My love. I came to My own
and My own didn't want Me, tossed Me out,
and crucified Me.
When you're rejected, you share My sufferings,
and those who suffer with Me reign with Me.
Don't think it odd that you're rejected.
The servant isn't greater than his lord.
I possess a treasure house of blessings
with your name on it. These blessings, lovingly
selected by Me just for you, will more than make up
for your grief.
Identify with Me and be strong. You and I
share a rare and beautiful intimacy.
You see, I took your disappointment, anguish, and grief
on My body on the cross.
Rejection has lost its power over you.

MATTHEW 27:35; 2 CORINTHIANS 4:9-10

May 16

Your greatest temptation is not the one
that solicits your consent to obvious sin,
but the one that hands you evil in the guise of good.
I want you to be wise and remove
the confusion between godliness and naïveté.
Good deeds are not always
what they seem.
Good deeds may take you
where I haven't called you,
and to people I haven't called you to.
I don't want you beguiled by the appearance
of good and temporary gratification.
I have so much better for you.
Wisdom and discernment will guide you
into that which is permanent
and blessed.
I want you blessed.

Proverbs 13:10; Ecclesiastes 2:13; John 16:13;
James 1:5

May 17

When you stand at a crossroad
in the throes of indecision,
examine carefully the implication
of your choices.
The first path is inked with
yesterday's familiar patterns.
The second path beckons with a tomorrow
shaded by the unknown.
The mean and lonely path with few rewards
requires the humblest heart,
and the path of sacrifice and starlit tears
can be the most blessed.
The hostile path of thorns and prayers
is the one for those who love the most.

The words *well done* from My throne,
more sublime than life itself,
sovereign, incomparable, unequaled,
are distanced only if stained
by the groans of fear and turning back.
The choice will be yours.

Jeremiah 6:16; Joshua 24:15; Hebrews 10:23;
Ephesians 3:12

May 18

If you gathered all your tears together in one place
and formed an ocean of them,
what name should we give
this great body of salty water?
If we called it simply *yours*,
that's how it'll remain: yours.
Your bitter sea will be all yours.
But! If you give your tears to Me,
the sea becomes Mine and I'll make it a blessing
to sail answered prayer upon.
Every earth-bound shrine comes to nothing
when it remains earth-bound.
Don't use your tears as a weapon or a
harbinger of doom.
Give them to Me gift-wrapped
as a love offering.

Isaiah 25:8; Psalms 56:8, 102:17, 116:8, 119:159

May 19

Loneliness is not so terrible, dear child.
My high calling for you
includes a certain amount of loneliness–
and also separation from sin
and removing yourself from the worldly pleasures
that wilt the heart and dry up the spirit.
You're My chosen one;
the old vacuous, cheap patterns of life no longer fit you.
You've thrown off the old ill-fitting coat
for your one-of-a-kind Holy Spirit designer robe.
Just look at you!
Loneliness won't last for long, dear one,
when you see in the spirit that you're surrounded
by a great and enormous cloud of delighted friends
as witnesses loving you and cheering you on.

Romans 1:1; 2 Corinthians 6:17; Ephesians 4:6;
Hebrews 12:1

May 20

Let Me hold you close to increase and renew
your enthusiasm and your love
for Me. Let Me love you and talk to you
in our sweet communion.
Don't be impatient in times of spiritual dryness–
be still and listen.
Hear what I have to say to you
and allow My consolations
to reach deep inside to the place where
you find yourself weary of spirit.
I never leave you or forsake you,
so when you feel bereft, alone, and
forsaken, it may be because of *your* distance
from Me, not *My* distance from you.
Come.
Climb into My arms today.

Psalms 23:2-3, 27:14; Isaiah 40:31; Mark 11:24;
Hebrews 13:5; Deuteronomy 7:8-9; 13

May 21

Never forsake
your high calling in Me
for the empty rewards
of those who bargain for your soul
with cheap offers, putrid and foul
in the stench of the sun.
Oh so tempting, the counterfeit promises are that
strangle your beauty, and kill your soul.
You're My chosen vessel,
My sweet adorable treasure.
I've chosen you for Myself
so together we can soar to high places,
dance on mountain tops,
sing with the angels,
thrill to the wonder of My creation,
and multiply everlasting joy.
Honor your calling, My beloved–
Stay close to Me.

Luke 15:13; 1 Corinthians 10:13; Acts 22:14;
James 4:7

May 22

Pause today to enjoy My created works.

Admire the glory of the sunrise,

and My painted sunset skies.

Look for the lonely evening star,

and observe Orion's royal command of night skies.

Can you listen for the roar

of the ocean's petulant waves,

the slippery ripple of the clear, stony brook?

Watch the grace of a swan in still water,

touch the horse's knitted mane,

hold the newborn baby and feel its breath on your chin?

I'm in every cell of every living creature,

and in every molecule you breathe.

I'm joyous in My creation, for it's all for you.

Today, let's celebrate life together.

PSALM 75:1

May 23

When you entertain the houseguest called self-pity,
you'll be left with a messy living room.
Self-pity is a thoughtless and solipsistic visitor;
it'll ruin your towels and eat all your food. It'll keep you up at
night
and wreck your stuff. Self-pity is a killer of joy;
it smells bad.
Self-pity is an unkempt pile of junk that rolls
out of garbage dumps, and chases your friends away.
Nobody wants to be friends with the person
who cohabits with self-pity.
Ugh!
Today, order self-pity out of your house and
out of your dear heart. Remember, I see everything,
and I know everything. I'm here every day
to load your life with benefits
and open My storehouses of goodness to you!
Put up the "No Vacancy" sign to self-pity today.

Psalms 23:5, 42:5, 68:19; Jonah 4:9-11;
Philippians 2:3-4; 1 John 3:16-17

May 24

Don't be too hungry for the world's adventure,
for easy affection,
for tasty morsels that vanish in the morning sun.
The pursuits for temporary pleasures
will entrap you and you'll squirm and kick
to get free, but the chains of bondage
are crushing.
Come to Me for a thrilling life,
for adventure beyond the world's offering.
Listen to Me and you'll live in
divine affection, embraced in the security
of My love.
In Me you're a new creation;
you're delivered from old sins
and so-called fun habits
that were out to shatter you.
You have a *new life* now
and a new hope.
You have an eternal exciting life in Me.
I've planted you securely in
My heart and My arms.

Proverbs 1:33, 21:17; 2 Corinthians 5:17;
Revelation 21:5

May 25

Pause, dear one,

and rest for a moment with Me.

When you pass through the valley of adversity,

your thoughts can contort and meander;

your energy can thin out and deplete,

but I'm here to lift you up.

I won't let you fall. I'll keep you in perfect peace

if you'll let Me.

I'll enliven and invigorate your mind.

Today, allow Me to breathe My sweet fresh breath

across your brow and stroke your dear cheek

with My peace. I'll restore quietness to your soul,

and renew your vision for the future.

My promises to you can't fail,

and for this reason you must lean into My arms

and rest.

Psalms 23:4, 29:11; Isaiah 26:3

May 26

I've loved you since the beginning.
I formed you in your mother's womb.
I knew you before you existed,
so you can trust that I know
what's best for you.
You can trust that I know
how to guide you into maturity
and build character in you
worthy of heaven's delight.
Love your life today
and appreciate
My hand leading you.
I'm appointing you to a place of safety
and contentment.
Many afflictions can beat at the doors
of My chosen ones,
but I deliver you from each threat.

PSALMS 34:19, 139:10; JEREMIAH 1:5

May 27

I'm sharpening your senses today so you'll
become sensitive to the exquisite view
from the crest of heaven's mountain,
and gaze down on the great life
I've called you to live.
Is the highest purpose of your life
to fulfill the purposes *I've* called you to?
Can you be happy in the knowledge
that *I'm* in control of everything?
The secret place of your strength
is to believe and trust *Me*
because your efforts
without Me are like dust in the wind.
With Me
all things are possible.
Today, allow Me to carry out My plans.
You do your part, and I'll do Mine.

PROVERBS 19:21; MATTHEW 19:26;
PSALMS 27:5, 91:1, 103:14; ISAIAH 64:6;
1 CORINTHIANS 2:7; PHILIPPIANS 4:13

May 28

Don't look back.
Hold Me close to your heart today
for I love you with a perfect love.
Look ahead
and envision the glorious future I've prepared for you.
You'll see that the present troubles
are in no way comparable to the glory ahead.
I'm leading you along the steep mountain roads
of faith. My Holy Spirit is composing
a living future life insurance plan
as we make the upward climb,
passing through the forest
of answered prayer.
Trees press their heads together
in approval as you continue *onward*,
not looking back.
This is living! Your future life insurance
is guaranteed with Me.

2 CORINTHIANS 2:14, 5:17; PSALMS 37:37, 84:12;
JEREMIAH 29:11

May 29

When you sing to Me
you present Me with your heart,
which I treasure.
Your songs of praise
are a wonderful and sacred gift
to Me, and they bring Me much joy.
There's a special castle in heaven
with hundreds of rooms
for you to fill with your songs of praise.
I love to join you in song. I dance about,
robes flying, laughing, and happy.
I stroke your head and rejoice when
you know Me for who I am.

PSALMS 69:30, 119:63, 104:33; 1 CHRONICLES 13:8

May 30

I love you with a love
that shaped the universe.
How delightful
is the dawn of your tender heart
toward Me.
I'm the lover of your soul.
Living in My love endorses your zeal
to accomplish more
and to prosper beyond the natural.
Because you love Me,
I give you the authority
to ascend the stairway of success,
for as your spirit soars,
so will the blessings abound around you
and your house.
Honor Me in all you do,
and I will do the rest.

1 John 3:1, 15:9; Romans 8:35; John 16:27;
Psalms 37:23, 122:7; Ephesians 2:4; Proverbs 6:22

May 31

Today, put an end to the shallow, polluted threats
of danger and doom that want to harass you.
Remember, I've given you a *new* mind to know
and live in the *truth*.
Remember, I've given you a purified, brilliant mind,
and this makes you smarter than the world.
I've made you so smart that when My thoughts of truth,
blessing, and empowerment enter you,
they rejuvenate every cell of your being,
and you become seriously happy.

PSALM 19:8; ROMANS 12:21

JUNE

"Not by might nor by power, but by my
Spirit," says the LORD Almighty.

ZECHARIAH 4:6, NIV

June 1

Be careful with your heart today.
The unruliness of the human heart
always seeks its own. Pleasure is the god
of the unrepentant, unruly heart.
But your heart surrendered to Me
has been made miraculously pure,
and it's kept that way by the power of your choices.
I've given you many spiritual gifts
to live your life triumphantly.
I've given you My Word to instruct, enrich,
and empower you to overcome every obstacle
and to rise up empowered with spiritual discernment
and understanding.
Your choices dictate the quality of your faith
and your level of intimacy with Me.
Pay attention to My invisible spiritual nudgings
and to My words today.
My written Word is your daily fortification
to guide the decisions of your heart.

Psalm 27:1-3; Romans 8:6-8, 14; James 4:8; 2
Thessalonians 3:3; Deuteronomy 30:19;
2 Corinthians 1:21-22

June 2

You're facing decisions, and today, as you face these decisions
you sense a pondering in the spirit, an uncomfortable
pinch in your belly–stop and listen. Don't be hasty with your
actions,
just listen. Observe.
I speak to you in many ways. Pay attention
to My invisible spiritual nudgings.
My Word is your daily fortification
to guide you in the decisions you make,
and when you feel ill at ease or confused,
pause and know that I want to help guide you.
What looks good may not always be the right choice.
Be aware that your flesh can be a dangerous influence, always
hungrily seeking its own gratification.
Be wise.
Take a Holy Spirit break.
Listen for My voice which you'll recognize
as I speak to your heart from a place deep inside you:
"*This* is the way. Walk in in it."

PROVERBS 14:12; 2 TIMOTHY 2:22; 1 JOHN 2:15-17;
ISAIAH 30:21; PSALM 27:14

June 3

Avoid being led by your emotions today.
Worldly circumstances, situations, and relationships
are best relegated to the realm
of My Holy Spirit for wisdom, guidance, and strength.
Stand strong today with firm footing,
solidly grounded in Me.
It's too convenient to take the easy route,
too easy to bow the knee
to circumstances and situations designed
to topple My child off the rock of faith.
I tell you, remain unshakably locked to Me!
Relationships may tug at your heart
to pull you away, but when you're solidly rooted in Me,
you won't wobble, wiggle, and topple,
no matter how tempting it may be.
There'll be trials and testing, but I promise you,
a resolute heart overcomes, and when your heart is fixed
on *our* relationship, you'll be stronger,
and more empowered.

Psalms 30:7, 57:7-11; Hebrews 13:5; John 16:33

June 4

In My stable of futures I have one just for you.
Here, climb onto the sleek, smooth back of your future.
I don't give your future
to chance and luck to ride.
Those with weak spiritual vision can't see their future.
Those with weak knees can't confidently mount their future.
Those toting backpacks of envy and greed
weigh too much for a peaceful ride on their future,
and angry riders topple off at the first trot.

If you saddle up your future with anger or resentment,
you'll gallop backward.
If you become frustrated and impatient,
your future will leave the trail and take off for the hills.
If you complain and insult your future,
you'll lope through the woods of life exhausted and
lost, forever hungry and wondering why.
Your future is yours to ride. Here are the reigns.
Chance and luck aren't in the saddle.
You are.

PSALMS 16:9, 33:18, 37:37; PROVERBS 14:30; ROMANS
15:13; JAMES 1:4; JEREMIAH 29:11

June 5

I want you to come out of your cave of self-pity today
and join the world of authentic people who have needs
just like yours.
I've got believers all over the world
on intimate terms with angels
who pray day and night,
and they'd like to pray for *you*.
I didn't call you to sit alone watching TV
feeling sorry for yourself and eating
food fit for badgers. You're My adorable child
and I love you!
I have a world out here for you
to love.

Psalms 43:5, 121:1-2, 131:2; Nahum 1:7; 1 Peter
1:8; Philippians 1:6

June 6

I have many things to show you,

many opportunities to give you,

many truths to reveal to you,

many gifts to offer you,

and miracles to bless you with.

The world is changing,

but I don't change.

Patterns of living are changing–

Mine don't change.

I want to show you things to come,

to prepare you to trust Me more.

I want you to know how to pray for results.

I want you to know how to prosper

through all circumstances.

Come close and give Me your attention

so I can lead and teach you to go higher.

LUKE 12:12; JAMES 1:17; PSALMS 32:8, 61:2;
ISAIAH 65:24

June 7

It's time to move on.
I have opened new doors for you.
I'm pouring out new opportunities
and new avenues of possibility in order to
unleash the well of creative expression
inside you.
Circumstances have kept you hidden
behind a wall of choices that seemed
to be right at the time, but now that wall is crumbling down,
setting you free, and the way ahead
is a spectacular
spiritual breakthrough.
Today, take that giant step
toward your radiant tomorrow.

PSALMS 34:21, 68:19, 73:28; LAMENTATIONS 3:22-24;
DEUTERONOMY 30:8; 2 CORINTHIANS 5:7, 17;
ACTS 1:8; JOHN 8:36

June 8

Give Me your best and your worst today.

Give Me your dreams.

Give Me your appetites and your hopes.

Give ALL to Me.

Trust Me to know what I'm doing.

I alone make your dreams come true,

and I alone know how to handle your appetites.

I turn your hopes to reality.

Be patient in this time of growth.

Step into this season with an open heart,

and give to Me what I deserve as your Lord.

Isaiah 12:2; Psalms 36:5, 91:2; Hebrews 10:23

June 9

I spiritually equip you for every situation.

You were born to overcome

and to rise up in wisdom in a transient world

where evil thrives like maggots on rotting meat.

Never be afraid of suffering.

You were born to rise above suffering.

You'll never totally eliminate pain or evil, dear child,

but you can eliminate your fears of pain and evil

and you can write the conclusion

to suffering's epic novel of your life.

Will it be a happily-ever-after ending?

Will it be "to be continued,"

or will you write the perfect finale

and live your days as the dynamic overcomer

I've equipped you to be?

1 Peter 4:12-13; James 5:10; 2 Corinthians 12:9;
John 16:33; Isaiah 61:7; Hebrews 2:10

June 10

I want you to be known as a strong person.
I want you to be known as one who can handle
suffering, snags, hindrances, troubles, and delays.
I want you to be full of My grace
to inspire and emanate goodness–
to live in honesty and handle the unmanageable,
calm the unruly, and love the unlovable.
You can't do these things in your human strength,
but you are spiritually equipped in all things
because you and I are *one*.
Don't miss the joy of discovering My gifts and abilities in you.

ZECHARIAH 4:6; PHILIPPIANS 4:13; 1 SAMUEL 2:9-10

June 11

Oh, I've been good to you.
I've answered the cries of your heart,
and I've blessed you with the kindness
of My heart.
I've extended My mercy to you,
I've showered you with goodness,
so that as My child you will feel infinitely secure
and resolutely happy.
Tell Me:
what are you going to do with
all the good things in your life today?

DEUTERONOMY 33:29; PSALMS 16:6, 23:1

June 12

When I make a promise
it's sealed at My throne.
It's *forever* and it can't be broken.
I tell you, your promise will come to pass
at its appointed time.
Don't reject the dream I gave you.
I'm training you to stand strong and to trust Me.
Don't be discouraged because it's taking time
for your dream to reach fulfillment.
The vision in your heart is true.
I placed it there!
I'm the author and the finisher of your faith,
and I authored your dream.
I began it and I'll complete it.
If I choose to wait
it's because I know what I'm doing.
The enemy of your soul
wants to overtake your mind with doubts.
Why don't you thwack him in the teeth
by trusting Me?

ROMANS 4:21; HEBREWS 6:12, 8:5, 12:2, 13:20;
JAMES 4:7; PSALM 18:30

June 13

Where My Spirit is, there's freedom
from the habits of the scarred and wounded soul.
Yes, I know habits are hard to break,
but let your habits be goodness, mercy,
love, justice, and a humble walk with Me.
Don't flop back into the life of bondage.
Don't start your old habits of obsessing
over evil done to you. Please.
If you slither about in the dung of yesterday's betrayals,
how will you see the beauty in this new day?
Forgiveness means if you're wronged,
stolen from, or lied about,
you forgive.
And if you're wronged, stolen from, or lied about again,
you forgive again.
And again.
Where My Spirit is, there's *freedom*.
Keep on forgiving and you'll love the transformation
in your heart and soul–you'll be *free*.

JOHN 8:36; ROMANS 8:2; COLOSSIANS 3:13;
MARK 11:25; GALATIANS 5:1

June 14

Live your life as a miracle today.
Even through the imperfection
and chaos around you,
live each moment as a unique event,
a miracle sent from Me just for you
to honor and revere.
Live each moment as if it were a lifetime.

There's life and purpose in every breath,
in every millisecond on earth.
Nothing in My kingdom
is without divine purpose,
and that is why this day and night
are important.
Make each moment live.

PSALMS 84:11, 107:8; COLOSSIANS 3:20-;
PROVERBS 8:35

June 15

I'm the LORD your God,
the holy one of Israel, your Savior.
I protect My own.
When you flop miserably in deep waters
gulping and gasping for air,
I won't let you drown,
and when you prance through fiery hoops
like an untrained tiger in a circus,
singeing your eyelashes and swallowing kerosene,
I won't let you go up in flames.
Today, all day, see yourself
as divinely and perfectly protected
no matter what river or circus
you've gotten yourself into.

ISAIAH 43:2-3

June 16

I'm here for you.

I'm your forever friend.

I'll never leave you or let you down.

If your father, mother, spouse,

son, or daughter forsake you,

I'll take you up.

I'll sustain you.

I'll comfort you.

Let Me encourage you

and defend you.

You can rely on My promises to turn

your mourning to unbridled, glad pleasure.

Your future is not dim with sizzled embers.

Be reassured

great things are yet to come.

PSALMS 27:10, 30:5, 103:6-8, 119:63, 147:3;
JOHN 15:15-16

June 17

Today,
don't impose a single limitation on Me.
Don't tuck Me behind the gates
of fear and faithlessness.
Let Me loose in your patterns of thought!
Free Me to speak to your ideas
and your vision for the future.
I've called you to an abundant life
where you can do all things through Me.
I've called you to live by faith,
not by old ideas based on doubt, suspicion,
or complacency.
You're beautiful to Me, and I want you to live
the wonderful full, rich life
I've planned for you.

Isaiah 54:10, 17; Romans 5:10; Matthew 6:8, 27;
John 10:10

June 18

Nothing is too small for Me
to make My own.
There's not a sigh too private
that I can't feel,
not a cell or microbe too small
for My presence to give it life.
I like to speak in a still, *small* voice,
but it's a voice that no crashing storm can muffle.
Can you hear Me in the song of a cricket in the night,
or in the precious yawn of a newborn child?
I'm in all things,
and it's the eye brightened by My Spirit
that knows this.
I've made your small, natural heart
a supernatural force,
now huge in the power of love.

ISAIAH 30:21; 1 KINGS 19:13

June 19

Today, be lifted up
above the problems that surround you
and your world.
Today, receive new vision,
new hope,
and new strength.
Don't limit Me and don't put a lid
on the blessings I have in store for you.
It takes courage to reach out
to the hope of the future
with an expanded vision. Your new season
begs a new vision,
one requiring more faith–
but as your vision enlarges,
so will your gifted ability to receive.

1 Peter 5:7; Psalm 23:4; Joel 2:28; Acts 19:2;
1 Chronicles 4:10

June 20

Today, discard your old ways of
thinking of ways to make things work out
the way you want them to.
I know all your needs before you do.
I've provided a full and rich life for you,
with every need met.
The new life I have for you cascades
with My blessings.
When you found Me, you found life.
Listen for My direction and follow
My instructions in My Word regarding
each detail of your life.
You'll be incredibly blessed
as you keep *My* ways,
and you'll begin to understand the immensity of
My favor.

Proverbs 8:32-35; Philippians 4:19; Hebrews 4:16

June 21

To know Me is to experience the sharpening of your senses.
The closer you grow to Me the deeper your awareness
will be.
No longer will you live in a fog with the world
buzzing around you in all its colors and motion
while you remain
unaware,
blind,
uncaring,
oblivious.
I'm waking the synapses and cells of your brain
that have lain dormant.
I'm stirring the portals of your consciousness,
and I'm making you aware and alive
like never before.
Today, tell yourself you're 100% alive!

Romans 6:11; Philippians 2:5; Colossians 3:2, 5;
Job 10:12; Proverbs 8:35; 1 Thessalonians 5:24

June 22

You're 100% alive
when you choose
to feel, think, see, hear, taste, touch
on purpose.
It means you experience the world around you
spiritually in tune,
and you *never* approach your day with a deadly
"whatever" attitude.
You dare to see the truth in all situations
with open eyes and holy discernment.
You don't waste your emotions
while spiritually empty.
Dear one, live your life to the fullest today!

Psalm 101:2; Jeremiah 33:3; Hebrews 11:6

June 23

I want you to stand on the crest of heaven's mountain

and gaze down at the great life

I've called you to live on the earth.

Can you see the fun ahead for you in My Spirit?

Can you see the blessings?

Can you see health,

friends,

love,

goodness,

mercy,

and prosperity ahead?

Do you see beautiful fellowship with Me?

Ah, open the eyes of your heart today,

and see.

Jeremiah 33:3; Deuteronomy 28:2, 6, 31:6;
Luke 10:23

June 24

I'm the great candle lighter.
I light the candle of your life.
The world I created was at first
without form and void, and I hovered
across the face of the deep with a great murmuring,
waiting to bestow Myself on the creation
and speak the words,
"Let there be light,"
because I am light.
If you're in need of insight
and understanding today,
call on My Spirit for illumination.
I'll dispel the darkness
so you can see clearly ahead.

PSALMS 18:28, 32:8; GENESIS 1:3; LUKE 1:79

June 25

There's light shining inside your soul today
and the people around you
will see Me in your eyes.
Your eyes are the windows of your
bright, incandescent soul, making you
alive in light and life.
Demons can't look you in the eye
because they're terrified by what they see.
All who hate this light will shrink from you,
but those who long for Me will find Me,
so be glad for the life-giving light in you.
Your brothers and sisters in Me will be blessed
when they look you in the eye,
and you'll party together with just one look.
Let it happen!

John 3:20-21, 8:12; Matthew 6:22; 1 John 1:7

June 26

It's your heart I see
and hear
and know,
so you can be confident, darling,
that I'm giving you
the desires of your heart today.
When you pray from the heart,
I know it because I live in your heart.
When your desires
are one with My Holy Spirit
you can trust Me to answer
because I'm the author of the desire.
I must answer
because your desire and Mine are one.
Don't be afraid to bring
every concern of your heart to Me.
Don't hold back.
It's our love for each other
that makes your wants
the same as Mine.

Philippians 2:13; Psalms 21:2, 37:3-5;
Romans 8:14; John 15:12-14

June 27

My name is greater than that of any name on earth
or in heaven and greater
than any assistance you might turn to.
So I tell you to pray in My name,
and My Father will answer. Be one with Me
and watch your life lift
to a higher dimension
of happiness and contentment this day.

Philippians 2:10; 1 Timothy 6:6;
Philippians 4:6-7

June 28

Does the battle feel too great for you today?
Remember, your strength comes from Me
and not from yourself or the world.
In your own energy you'll falter
as quickly as it takes a drop of water
to drip from a sprout. *Splat!* and you're
ready to quit.
I've made you capable of accomplishing much
with the many natural gifts I've given you,
but without Me, those very gifts
can be misused because you were born
to know and serve Me, not yourself.
So on the battlefield of life today,
be brave. Lean into My arms, take a deep breath,
and let's start over.
Feel My strength pour into your body and soul,
revitalizing you.
Your battle has already been won
because I've won it for you.

Psalms 18:39, 48-49, 24:8, 37:34;
Deuteronomy 33:27; Isaiah 59:19

June 29

Be kind, dear one.

It's true I've called you to be strong

and to conquer difficult obstacles.

True, I've called you to rise up tough and resilient

in a sin-conscious world.

And I'm also calling you to be kind.

You can win an argument by bulldozing

over your opponent; you can punch and kick your way

to success; you can lay flat those in your life

with a will of their own,

or you can be kind.

You're strong when you're considerate.

You're tough when you're humble.

You're brave when you're gentle.

Kindness never boasts, nor is rude in any way.

I am kindness.

Be like Me.

PSALM 18:35; PROVERBS 19:22; EPHESIANS 4:32;
MATTHEW 11:29; PHILIPPIANS 2:1-2;
2 CORINTHIANS 1:22

June 30

Be patient, beloved. Just as you can't force open the bud of a
flower,
that must bloom in its own time, so must you persevere
and enjoy this time to marvel, admire and be in awe
of the blooming process in you, like the life within
the bud quivering to spring forth; like the stretching,
yearning,
and incubating before it finally realizes its purpose
and becomes what it was meant to be
from the beginning.

Watch how the deepening colors of the bud grow iridescent
as its leaves reach out to gather more sky into their veins.
Now see the petals expand, their smiling faces upturned from
the earth.
I welcome them, whole and complete.
I watch *your* petals unfolding now,
and this blossoming of yours, My darling, is a process
that can't be rushed. *Cherish this time.*

JAMES 1:4; ISAIAH 35:1-2

JULY

For the LORD God is our sun and shield;

He gives us grace and glory.

The Lord will withhold no good thing

from those who do what is right.

PSALM 84:11, NLT

July 1

Who is the one who reaches the peaks
of high mountains?
Who climbs the distant side
of the treacherous cliffs
where an unstable toe-hold could
lead to death?
Who dares such a climb
enduring storms, thirst, hunger,
pain, and exhaustion,
and doesn't give up until reaching the top?
I'll tell you who.
It's the one who *has trained* for the climb.
What about you?
The higher calling boot camp of My Holy Spirit
is taking registrations now.
Are you preparing to climb above
the sharp ridges of trial and loss,
and invest in the solid foothold of higher calling *faith*?
Have you packed your higher calling faith gear?
Or do you prefer hanging out in the spongy pap
of low land spinelessness?
The mountain waits.

Revelation 12:11; Luke 10:19; Ephesians 3:16-17, 6:10;
Colossians 1:10-12; Isaiah 40:29;
2 Corinthians 5:7; 1 Peter 1:7-9

July 2

Place today's needs in My hands, dear one.
Place the concerns of your heart and mind in My care.
Where your heart is, there you'll find your treasure.
Have you examined My wildflowers lately?
Have you taken a good look at the design
of the landscape of My healthy earth?
No visual wonder compares to what I have created,
yet you won't find a single rose, fern, or pine
worried about how they look. And the lilies!
I tell you, no wealth in the world can buy
the wardrobe of the lilies. Yet they don't do a lick of work.
Look at the birds of the air. Do they mope and brood?
No! Yet not one of them plants or harvests;
they don't fret about their appearance,
nor do they stress at the shortness of their lives.
If I clothe the grass of the field, the hawk, the rose,
the lilies of the valley, how much more do I clothe
and care for you?
Don't you understand, My darling?
I created everything for *you*.

Romans 1: 20; Luke 12:22-31, 34;
Genesis 1:22, 26, 28

July 3

You've always been in My heart.

There isn't one instant of your life

that I haven't watched over.

While you were in your mother's womb,

I promised you unconditional love.

I knew there would be times

of rejection,

sorrow,

and betrayal.

I knew you'd feel unwanted and unloved at times,

and I loved you even more.

I made a promise to you from your mother's womb

that you'd be perfectly loved forever,

and you're living that promise today.

PSALMS 37:18, 23, 71:6, 73:26; PHILIPPIANS 4:19;
JOHN 10:27-28

July 4

The rewards I have for you are above and beyond
fickle human hurrahs and flattering puffery.
When you're one with Me
our achievements party around us
as bejeweled heroes.
I've told you there's little satisfaction
in achievements apart from Me.
The attention you earn from the world
will flutter away like feathers in the wind,
and be forgotten,
But *our* relationship blooms forever,
and the accolades you receive from Me
will sparkle on heaven's hall of fame for eternity,
and the partying won't ever end.

2 Corinthians 4:18; Matthew 25:21-23;
Daniel 12:3; Isaiah 51:11; Romans 8:38-39

July 5

I've loved you from the very foundation of the world,
which tells you how long I've known you.
I had a purpose for your life long before
you were conceived.
You've only known Me since you gave your life
to Me, but I've known you since creation.
Ponder it.
Do you think I know you well enough
to know what's best for you?
Do you believe I'm concerned
about the details of your days?
Do you ever think how happy you make Me
when your life, which I gave you, bursts with joy in Me?
I love it when you turn to Me
with a shout of thanks, and I'm deeply moved
when I see you plunge forward,
risking all to help someone who's in deeper need than you.
I love answering your prayers.

PSALMS 22:9-10, 32:8; EZRA 3:11; HEBREWS 4:16;
JOHN 8:31-32, 15:7; COLOSSIANS 3:23-24

July 6

Love Me today in simplicity,
and give everything you do to Me.
Your gifts to Me are a joyful fragrance
to My nostrils.
I see your dear face knowing you're Mine
and I tell you, your adoring heart
is as precious to Me as a thousand festivals
of praise in My honor.
You bring Me much delight.

Talk to Me.

Listen to Me.

Worship Me.
And you'll live the most exciting life on earth.

Luke 21:1-3; Song of Songs 6:4; Jeremiah 15:20;
Colossians 3:17; Zechariah 4:6

July 7

Do you know how beautiful you are to Me,
and how I long to speak to you?
Do you know how precious
these quiet moments with you are to Me?
With just one moment with Me,
you'll know more contentment in your soul
than days and nights of the fun and pleasure
the world has to offer.
Your good works and skills can't accomplish
the pleasure of one moment alone with Me.
One moment of your busy day
to enter into the presence of complete perfection
sitting at the center of My sheltered peace–
isn't this the best moment of all?
I want this sacred time with Me to be your foundation
of each day.

Proverbs 31:30; Philippians 4:7; Ecclesiastes 9:17;
Psalm 4:4; 1 Corinthians 2:10-12; John 14:9;
Colossians 2:9-10; Matthew 7:24

July 8

Inner beauty can be counterfeited for a time,
but then the core of the soul is exposed–
the temper erupts like Mt. Etna,
the snake emerges to steal or lie,
and later, of course, excuses are made.
You say you're just tired, you're sorry.
O My child, I forgive and I forgive,
but I want you to know that My personality
can become part of yours with an eternal quality that's
glorious and indestructible,
and where temptation and lack of discipline
won't continually overtake you.
No moment's agitation
will spoil your sweetness,
nor will every irritation pollute your composure.
You won't be tempted to steal
what belongs to someone else.
Your inner beauty is the reflection
of the moments and hours
you spend with Me.

PROVERBS 14:29, 31:30; JAMES 1:19;
HEBREWS 2:18; SONG OF SONGS 4:1, 7;
1 CORINTHIANS 13:12; GALATIANS 4:6, 5:22-26

July 9

Today, use your holy microscope
to discover a world bigger than the one
you're tempted to take for granted.
Be wild. Gaze into the flickering eyes of birds
and ask them for their stories.
Kiss the smiling faces of the lily, iris, and rose.
Clap your hands with the trees who love to
praise their Master. Listen for the song in rocks.
Name the crustaceans on the ocean floor.
Dance barefoot on the sofa.
Lighten up.

PSALMS 8:3, 9:1, 144:15

July 10

A good conscience is one
that's armed with truth,
and one that won't settle for an easy route
through the thorny patches of life.
A good conscience doesn't emanate from
an emotionally impoverished soul.
A good conscience devours My Word
like a person starving.
A good conscience refuses to make excuses
for what it knows is wrong.
A good conscience doesn't continue to
eat forbidden fruit which makes
the whole world sick.
A good conscience won't steal
just because it's convenient.
A good conscience doesn't take credit
where it's not due.
A good conscience hates lies and
hypocrisy, and will never be seen cavorting with
deceit and trickery.
A good conscience won't trot betrayal's avenues
of flim-flam recklessness because a good conscience
is above all loyal and sincere.
Today, think about these things.
Think about the value of your good conscience.

HEBREWS 9:14, 13:18; ACTS 24:16; ROMANS 9:1;
2 CORINTHIANS 1:12, 4:2; TITUS 1:15

July 11

Dare to be a happy person today.

Dare to be strong.

Dare to overcome!

A good conscience is one that rejoices in truth,

ever confident, and is at peace in adversities.

A strong person must have a good conscience.

An overcomer in My kingdom

can't overcome without a good conscience.

A good conscience is like fine polished gold,

A good conscience is a delight to Me.

2 Corinthians 1:12; 1 Thessalonians 5:8;
Ephesians 6:10-11; Revelation 3:21;
Hebrews 10:22; 1 Timothy 1:5

July 12

Consider yourself blessed.
Nothing can take away
the sweet blessings that are yours alone.
Consider yourself free from everything
that has tried to hold you down
or hurt your feelings.
Consider yourself a new person inside and out.
The hurts of the past can't control you today.
You have a new life now,
and a new heart that I fill with happiness
and fresh wonder and excitement.
Discover today that your world
is chock-full of delightful surprises,
and you're more blessed than you can imagine.

EPHESIANS 1:3; 2 CORINTHIANS 5:17, 9:8;
PSALMS 68:19, 103:1-5, 107:9; PROVERBS 22:1;
JEREMIAH 31:14; JOEL 2:26

July 13

It's a day to be humble.
Take Me with you everywhere you go.
I'll calm your fluctuating nerves;
I'll guide you
and remind you of the humble walk.
I'll give you a loving poke
if you act self-righteously
or insist on your own way.
I'll gently nudge you if you boast
or behave with self-importance.
I'll lift you up so you can see
the path of true fulfillment and recognize
the itsy-bitsy bite-sized life when
it's dominated by pride.
Be humble and drop pride's grubby grip on you
in order to gain the whole world
and the wonderful years I have for you.

MICAH 6:8; MARK 8:35, 10:43; 1 TIMOTHY 6:17;
PHILIPPIANS 3:8-9

July 14

Who vindicates you in every courtroom of life?
Who's your most reliable helper in times of need?
Who is always there–
protecting you,
embracing you in perfect love?
Your employers?
Your pals?
Who hears your cries in the night and comforts you?
Who lifts you up when you fall down?
Who calls you *beloved*?
Your dentist?
Your physician?
Your lawyer?
Hmm?
Remember, dear child,
the things and the people you now think are immutable
will one day be gone, like fluff in the wind.
Success is temporary, riches are fleeting,
but I am from everlasting to everlasting.
I never change.
Today, think about this. I love you.

1 Timothy 6:17; Psalms 121:1-4, 138:7, 148:13-14;
Nahum 1:7; 1 John 4:16

July 15

Wherever you go,
I'll clear the way for you.
Whatever you need, I'll provide.
When you step out and declare My name
I'll favor your cause.
Know that what concerns you concerns Me.
The tribulation in the world shall not alarm you
but instead, bring you
to your prayer station where you take down
strongholds and declare My Word
and will into every situation.
You'll avoid fretful talk
and divisive babble. You'll pray from your
heavenly position of authority
and confident assurance. You'll never forget
I am exalted
above all principalities and powers!

1 John 5:14-15; Ephesians 2:6; Philippians 2:5-11;
Luke 10:19; John 15:16

July 16

Gossip?
Show Me gossip
and I'll show you dried weeds
and cracked, parched mud.
Gossip can paddle the air in the guise
of prayerful concern or even
godly correction.
Put Me before you,
and you won't succumb
to troublesome words of derision
against someone else.
People may belch out insults
like dirty rain,
and they may slash at My little ones
with sarcasm and ridicule,
but every curse shall boomerang back
at the sender.
That is why *you* too
must keep yourself pure today
and don't allow gossip
to spurt from your beautiful mouth.

Isaiah 54:15, 17; Jeremiah 32:17, 27; Proverbs 26:2;

Psalms 19:14, 59:7, 9-10; Ephesians 4:29

July 17

Look where you're standing.

You're standing on Me. I'm your rock.

Your enemy, the devil, is sneaking around your feet

like a desperate, hungry animal looking for someone

without self-control to chew on.

Be aware.

Be alert.

Be authentic.

If you lie to yourself about your habits, and

lose control over your day,

if you're easily tempted,

don't lose a second, *hang onto the rock.*

I, Christ Jesus, am the rock for you to stand on

with absolute confidence

and security.

I'm your escape from the devil and yourself!

1 Peter 5:8, 9; Galatians 5:16; 1 Corinthians 10:12

July 18

Don't say you have no power.

Be like the prophet who proclaimed,

"As for me, I am filled with power,

with the spirit of the LORD,

and with justice and might!"

Isn't that beautiful?

Can you, like Micah, proclaim the truth today?

I've armed you with strength,

that'll never run out.

You'll soar on wings like eagles,

you'll run and not grow weary,

you'll walk and not faint.

Proclaim it!

Proclaim the truth to your heart,

and out of My glorious riches, I'll strengthen you

with the power you need.

Never say you have no power.

MICAH 3:8; ISAIAH 40:31, 41:10;
EPHESIANS 3:16-17; ACTS 1:8

July 19

Today, concentrate on the task I've given you,
and don't allow yourself to be deterred
and get off track because of interferences
that don't concern you.
If others annoy or raise a quarrel with you,
step back and take charge of your heart.
Selfish ambition will kick you in the shins
even if you win the argument.
It's not smart to rush into someone else's squabble.
In fact, a person who meddles
in a quarrel not his own
is like one who seizes a dog by the ears.
Use your gift of wisdom today
and don't be distracted.

PROVERBS 3:30, 20:3, 26:17; 1 CORINTHIANS 12:8;
PHILIPPIANS 2:3; HEBREWS 12:14

July 20

Do you think I'm taking too long
to answer your prayers?
I see you there in the valley of patient waiting
and you're getting anxious.
You're wondering when? When? When?
The valley of patient waiting
is crowded with toe-tapping, finger-thrumming
believers asking the same question.
Patience comes with a price, dear one.
You can't order it from a catalog
like a new skin cream or a wonder-vitamin pill.
Patience requires courage.
You must have courage to wait, believing
I know what I'm doing.
I never go back on a promise,
and I will surely answer you.
But please don't forget, I answer in My time,
not yours.

Isaiah 25:9, 56:9, 65:24; Psalm 91:15

July 21

Consider your friends today.
When Moses, during battle, grew weary
holding the rod of victory high,
who was it who held up his hands?
Aaron and Hur held up Moses' hands,
one on one side, and one on the other
so he'd remain steady and strong.
Friends will do this for you.
So let Me ask you, what can you do to be a blessing
to *your* friends today?
You were born to love
and be loved.
Can you hold weak arms up in prayer?
Do you have a kind, generous word
ready to share?
What can you do to comfort and encourage?
A friend is compassionate, sympathetic,
humble and faithful.
Today, be a friend.

Proverbs 17:17, 27:10; Exodus 17:12; 1 Peter 3:8;
1 Samuel 18:1

July 22

Be filled with hope today!
Take hold of hope as never before
and know that the Maker of heaven and earth,
the Ruler of the seas, the earth,
and all there is,
loves you and is faithful to you.
Hopelessness is the result of a lie,
and a lie lasts only moment
because a lie can't hold substance
in the dynamic life-giving atmosphere
of truth. Lies that rob you of hope are worms
that disintegrate in light.
You are a child of light;
the lie disintegrates, *Puff!* like that.
The truth lasts forever.
I'm telling you today to proclaim the truth
of My promises in your life.
I promise I'm near you. I hear you.
My promises to you are your reality.

Romans 8:24; Hebrews 6:18, 11:1; Psalm 146:6

July 23

Where do you run for safety?
Your bed?
Under the table?
Behind Mamma's skirts?
Or do you rush into My heavenly high tower
where I've promised eternal safety?
When you're desperate,
where do you head for help?
To the pharmacy,
the supermarket,
next door?
Or do you immediately take off
for the banquet hall of mercy,
where angels welcome you to your most sacred
holy refuge?
Oh, don't forget the one who loves
to help you.
Through thick and thin, I'm here every day
as your stronghold and your God,
endlessly loving you.

PSALMS 18:2, 59:9, 16-17, 144:2, NAHUM 1:7;
2 SAMUEL 23:14; HEBREWS 4:16; PROVERBS 21:21

July 24

Who has gathered up the wind in the hollow of his hand?

Who has wrapped up the sea in the pocket of his coat?

Who has established the borders of the earth?

Tell Me if you know, dear child.

It's I who rules the surging sea,

and when its waves mount up,

I quiet them. I rebuke the wind and the lightning;

the hail, snow, and clouds do My bidding.

I still the turmoil of nations and I make

the loud voice of the fool a mere vapor.

Listen. I am the Lord of *all*,

and I gave the oceans their boundaries

so the waters wouldn't overstep My command.

I'm the one who marked the foundations of the earth–

And I can work a miracle in your life today.

Never underestimate Me.

PSALMS 65:5-7, 89:9, 107:29; MATTHEW 8:26;
PROVERBS 30:4; PHILIPPIANS 4:19

July 25

I've been talking to you since before you were born.
I'm the first one who welcomed you into the world
when your mother gave birth.
I've loved and cherished you forever,
and yet you haven't always been aware of My presence.
How many times do you think Moses trekked past Me
with his sheep before he noticed
the inextinguishable bush on fire in the sand?
How long do you suppose I had to call out to Moses
before he heard Me?
I tell you, My presence is subtle, unpredictable,
and supernatural. A burning bush, a mighty wind,
a silent cave, a grassy patch beneath a tree,
the solemn privacy of the holy of holies,
and dear one, in the sacred halls
of your own heart–that's where you'll find Me.
Absorb these words I'm speaking to you,
and come climb into My heart.

Psalm 71:6; Exodus 3:2; 1 Kings 19:9-12;
Luke 1:8-15; Acts 2:1-2

July 26

Acquire wisdom, and with all your acquiring,
get understanding.
If you're wise,
wisdom will reward you.
You won't find happiness
without wisdom.
Wandering about looking for happiness
in the toothsome grins of strangers and flatterers,
eating the deceptive sweetmeats of ambition,
and dancing in the footprints of prideful learning
will never make you happy.
You belong to Me.
I am your happiness
I am wisdom.
Wisdom will delight your soul
and pour healing oil on your parched, dry heart.
Wisdom will bless your life with treasures
of happiness money can't buy.
As you gain wisdom and understanding
accessing My instruction and direction,
all things will be added to you.
and you'll become more and more like Me.

Proverbs 3:13, 4:7; Psalm 51:6; Matthew 6:33;
Colossians 3:10

July 27

Think of yourself today
as an artist.
You're a painter
preparing your canvas and brushes
for a monumental invasion of color,
shape, and movement,
creating what the world has never seen.
Think of yourself as possessing
skills to amaze
with your original expressions of love
and fearlessness.
Every stroke you make on your canvas of life
is yours and yours alone. You're the one
who chooses the colors, the viscosity,
and the movement of the brush. It's you
making the art, nobody else.
Are you glad for the artist
I made you to be?
Are you thankful today that you're
one-of-a-kind, an original,
and that what you bring to the world
is wonderful?

PSALM 139:14; GENESIS 1:22; EPHESIANS 5:20;
COLOSSIANS 3:10

July 28

Today, think of yourself
as a sculptor
facing your block of stone
and all ready to chisel out the beauty
locked inside.
A form in the stone has been waiting
to be set loose for centuries,
and My Father has sent you
to set the stone-trapped captive free.
You've been given the gift to see
into the hard interior of stone.
You're blessed with the consecrated skill
required to create beauty from ashes.
Trust your gifts today.
Trust Me who made you *who you are.*
Dare to chisel away
at your divinely appointed task
with dignity and holy pride.

Ephesians 4:1; Isaiah 61:3; 2 Timothy 1:9;
Romans 11:29

July 29

Think of yourself today
as an architect
at the drawing board of life
drawing your blueprints for a new environment
where learning, joy, and love will prevail.
See yourself flowing in your builder's gifts
moving forward with the dream
I put in your heart.
I tell you, create with confidence and enthusiasm,
and don't hold back. I am with you to bring to pass
the results of what I've birthed in you.
Execute your plans with the skill
I've gifted you with,
and you'll receive approval and favor,
and many lives will be saved, enriched,
and prepared for the days to come.

PROVERBS 24:27; DANIEL 12:3; JOHN 14:12

July 30

Today,
think of yourself
as a musician
born to bring heaven's music
to a world weary of noise.
The beautiful song is yours,
yours alone to release into the atmosphere
of My creation
and to resound it against the raucous-topped mountains
and the sky's lustrous silver linings.
No gift of Mine is given without
the love of all heaven
as its back-up cheering it on.
A song without love is not found
in heaven's banks of hymnals and scores.
No recording's ever made it
to heaven's shopping cart without
My love.
So here's your question for the day:
As My personal adorable musician,
bringing music only you can make to a cacophonous world,
doing exactly as I created you to do,
and being exactly who I created you to be,
are you grateful you're you?

PSALM 7:17, 30:12, 33:3; 2 CHRONICLES 5:13;
EXODUS 15:1; JEREMIAH 33:11; ISAIAH 38:20, 49:13;
COLOSSIANS 3:15

July 31

I want you to love your life
and stop with the complaints and grievances
which are like annoying bug bites.
Discontent is a swollen itch
that you live with day by day,
and no swab of happy lotion will help.
You'll go on scratching through the nights
and finding even more to complain about.

I have a sweet contentment cream
like a warm massage to cover you
from head to toe, and mellow your heart.
This balm is all yours if you'll open the door
of your disenchanted mind
where I'm standing and knocking.
Let Me in!
I come with new comforting words
to replace the sore complaints that bristle and scratch
at you. I have beautiful things to tell you!
Let Me in and I'll restore your faith
and give you delicious peace today.

PHILIPPIANS 4:11; REVELATION 3:20; PSALM 51;
1 TIMOTHY 6:6; JOHN 16:33

AUGUST

Let all the earth fear the LORD;

Let all the inhabitants of the world

stand in awe of Him.

For *He* spoke, and it was done;

He commanded, and it stood fast.

PSALM 33:8-9, NASB

August 1

I created you to go forward into this day
with great openness of heart,
and to embrace life fully.
If a dark moment emerges
in the sunlight of the hours,
breathe a prayerful thank you
and listen for My voice whispering
in your sweet ear:
It is well.
If an enemy of your peace strikes,
I'll give you a warrior's courage to rise up
and take a swing at the ugly thing in My name.
Don't lose a moment in discontent
or defeat today. Embrace goodness.
My Spirit embraces you.

2 THESSALONIANS 3:3; PSALM 73:28; LUKE 10:19;
EPHESIANS 6:10-13; PHILIPPIANS 1:6

August 2

Don't avoid life's difficult paths.

Experience the pain

and be complete. Be whole.

Exercise your muscles.

I'll not have you weak

and pampered like a fat rabbit.

Enter through the eye of hard work,

like the narrow hole

at the end of a needle.

Go through

singing and chuckling as you go.

Be wise. Be sympathetic.

Never be afraid of the thief in the night.

Be prepared.

Have a sense of humor.

Your faith is your armor.

Your wit is your relief.

Your courage is your strength.

JAMES 1:2-4; LUKE 10:19, 13:24; MATTHEW 19:24;
EPHESIANS 6:10, 13-16; PSALMS 18:2, 119:71

August 3

Nothing is insignificant to Me.
Listen to the sweet urgings of My will
for this new day.
Quiet your heart.
Listen for our hearts to melt together
because I am in the silence,
and I want you to cherish the simplicity
of this moment.
I want you to observe the miniscule,
the almost imperceptible,
touch of My hand on the world
around you.
It's the restless, immature soul that demands
the grand, noisome, and monumental
at all times.
Cherish the simple
to keep from the fermentation of impatience.
Train your spirit to listen for Me
in the silent, desolate spaces.

Isaiah 30:15; Psalms 46:10, 62:5, 69:32, 104:25;
1 Peter 3:4; James 4:10; Zechariah 4:10

August 4

You're giving too much time
to what is now gone.
The past offers you nothing but more of itself.
When you obsess about the past,
you give it power to rule the present
and you miss the glory of *this* moment.
To pine for yesterday's riches
is as destructive to the soul
as resentment for what's been robbed.
I tell you, today choose to appreciate
and open your eyes to the goodness in your life
as it is right now.
I use the past, both good and bad, as an instrument to create
a greater future.
I see your past as not only healed and delivered
from the gnawing teeth of the devil,
but as a scrapbook of success to add new pages to.
You're a living wonder today.
Think in terms of today, as I do,
and give the past in its many dimensions
to Me. I know how to turn everything to good.

Song of Songs 2:11; Proverbs 2:20-21; Job 1:4;
Psalm 30:5; Isaiah 58:8; Romans 8:28

August 5

Be strong today.
When things seem dreary
and without hope,
grab hold of the strength
I've poured into you.
The notion of hopelessness
doesn't exist in My Kingdom,
and I've given you the spiritual strength
to combat every wily scheme aimed at you
to discourage and tear down your faith.
The substance of everything you hope for
is positioned in your faith.
Be strong, I tell you.
Prove the power of My might today!

PROVERBS 24:5; HEBREWS 11:1; 1 TIMOTHY 6:12;
PSALM 68:35; EPHESIANS 6:10

August 6

Today, dear one,
the subtle taste of jealousy
may try to pinch your cheeks
and cause a grinding of your teeth,
but I want you to be prepared. Pull back
your shoulders and chop the temptation
away with the sword of My Word.
No temptation can grab you by the ear
and yank you into its dark hole
without your help.
Jealousy does more than cause sores on the tongue:
it's a killer.

PHILIPPIANS 2:3; JAMES 4:2; SONG OF SONGS 8:6;
1 CORINTHIANS 10:13; PROVERBS 27:4;
GALATIANS 5:14-15

August 7

I see you chartered on the open sea of faith
knowing My eyes are on you,
knowing My anchor holds in every storm
no matter the condition of your ship.
You're older now—you've sailed through
some furious storms with your mainsails tattered
and your weatherboard bruised and beaten.
And you've also cruised along the calm waters
of faith singing songs of deliverance and thanks,
knowing there's no storm that can
rip the fluke, pull up your anchor, flood your deck,
tear apart the bow, eat up the chine,
and swallow you whole.
I've kept you safe in the storm
and you'll stay safe all your life.

Job 26:12; Isaiah 4:6; Psalm 107:29; Proverbs 1:33

August 8

Mark your calendar:
Today, I will not get upset.
I'm right at your side
with more than enough peace
to silence your emotional tsunami.
Think of yourself as a runner.
All of your hard work, practice, and sacrifice
is put to the test as you bring your very best
to the race of a lifetime.
But! Your opponent gains speed
in the final fifteen yards,
and crosses the finish line first.

When someone else succeeds
at nabbing the trophy you thought was yours,
find grace in your heart
to appreciate their success.
Contention and jealousy are evil cousins
who corrupt the minds of good people.
Always walk away from jealousy.
Tell yourself no one is less worthy than you.

1 Corinthians 9:24; Proverbs 17:14;
2 Corinthians 12:20; Galatians 5:26;
John 13:34; Mark 10:43-44

August 9

I want you to learn when to contest
and when to keep your spiritual fists
to yourself.
I'm speaking to you of discernment–
spiritual discernment is a gift of My Holy Spirit
and it means you must give permission
for My will to cohabit your will
in penetrating light
that gives you clear vision on all sides
of what's before, behind, above, and around you.
There's a time to fight and a time not to fight.
The gift of discernment tells you when to speak
and when not to speak,
when to act and when to remain still.
The gift of discernment sheds light on what's true
and what's false.
The gift of discernment allows you to see through
the veil of unknowing and confusion,
and to recognize evil spirits.
Pray for, receive, activate, and put to use
My Holy Spirit's gift of discernment
today and every day of your life!

ZECHARIAH 10:5; ECCLESIASTES 3:5;
1 CORINTHIANS 1:12; ACTS 27:9-10

August 10

It may not be easy to watch someone else
walk off with the promotion or accolades
you deserve.
It may not be easy when another
takes possession of the blessings you've prayed for
and not received.
If you feel set aside and passed over when others
get the recognition and breakthrough,
rejoice for them. Be glad.
Remember, I look at your
heart, and it's your heart I love and promote.
I don't compare you with any living soul,
I see you as *you*. Never envy another.
Your day is coming.

Job 5:2; Proverbs 14:30; 1 Corinthians 13:4;
Colossians 3:12

August 11

My daily words to you
are meant to guide you
into My profound mysteries
and your assignment on earth.
I want you to be attentive to all I tell you.
Drink in My words
and become a simmering arrow
dipped in the fire of faith
that shoots a direct bull's-eye
into the heart of My purposes.
By My Word you can move mountains.
By My Word the sick are healed,
the lame walk,
the blind see.
Today, realize you were born
to do on earth as I did.

1 CORINTHIANS 2:9; PSALM 40:8; ISAIAH 46:10;
PROVERBS 1:23; ROMANS 11:33

August 12

You worry about the events in the world,
the horrors of the past with nation against nation,
and evil running rampant on the earth.
Listen to Me.
No atrocity performed on earth escapes My eye.
Man's inhumanity to man is not too heinous for Me
to break the neck of its master. I alone hold the power
to destroy the powers of evil with My fist of judgment,
but this is *My* work, not yours.
You, My darling, pray
and do good in your sphere of influence.
I've shown you the power of goodness, and what I require
of you. Love mercy, do justly,
and walk humbly with Me.
With these, you'll change the world.

REVELATION 19:6; PSALMS 88:2, 98:3; MICAH 6:8

August 13

Be sensitive today to My presence
in the world around you.
Allow My Spirit to awaken your senses
to the sublime
and to all natural beauty.
Loving My world is a form of humility
as you set your inner conflicts aside
to communicate with life outside yourself.
Put your hands on the earth; experience its pulse.
Smell the rose with deeper appreciation, and dare to
watch the scurrying of the ant with greater amusement.

Delight in the dance of sunlight against your sleeve.
Be awed at the divine artwork a river of rain
makes as it slides across a window pane.
Feel the wind on your cheek
as the kiss of a friend you miss.
Don't lose out on the anthem of a sunset
because the drumbeat of worry has deafened you
to the wonders of your world,
and you fail to hear the sigh of My love.

PSALM 66:1-4; SONG OF SONGS 7:12, 8:13

August 14

To do one thing without Me is unnatural for you,
and exceedingly lonely.
I am He who fashioned the heavens.
I am He who stretched the waters into the seas,
and I am He who created you to be My *friend*.
The heavens tremble and the seas roar,
but with you, My child, I like to sit down
and relish a holy conversation.
I want to hear you speak of urgent earthly matters
and of your compassionate love
for the issues, troubles, and people I love.
I want to show you great and wonderful things
from heaven's storehouses of answered prayer.

Genesis 1:1, 20; Deuteronomy 10:14, 28:8;
Exodus 33:1; John 15:5; Psalm 91:1, 15;
Proverbs 15:8, 16:7, 22:11; Isaiah 46:10

August 15

If you have ears to hear,
I'll speak to you now.
It's far easier to admire and make heroes
of those you've never met
than someone in your own midst whose foibles
you know only too well.
It's far more convenient to be kind
to a troubled stranger
than to be compassionate toward
an annoying soul of your own household.
Is there an aggravating, prickly someone
you might speak a gracious word to today–
someone you might make feel appreciated and less alone?

JAMES 1:8; ROMANS 12:9; PSALM 151:5;
MATTHEW 5:46

August 16

Love is at the root of all I am,
and I want you to learn love's language.
I want you to spend time meditating
on My love
and in the practice of loving.
Love is not an accident
of good will or of genial pleasantries.
Love is deeply selfless,
penetrating through the heated,
throbbing core of every universe.
My holy love ignores no human being
nor any human suffering,
and I extend mercy which often the human eye
can't perceive.
Always know: love ignores no one,
insults no one,
takes no one for granted,
refutes no one,
crushes no one.
In the perfection of My love, there is perfect life.
There is nothing greater.

Romans 5: 1; John 4:7-11, 16:24; Isaiah 30:18-19;
1 Corinthians 13:4-10; Proverbs 10:12;
Matthew 5:48

August 17

I want to take the heavy burdens from you today.
I want to teach you the skills of *rest*,
and how to leap into My loving kindness
like plunging into refreshing cool waters
on a blistering hot day.

Don't ignore My offer to pass
your burdens and cares over to Me
because frustration and exhaustion
will come to sink your ship of hard work,
and you'll be too tired to send them away.
Come to Me now with every burden
and the pressures of your life's circumstances
will subside and recede into My care.

Rest, dear one. I'm reviving and energizing you.
In the midst of the storm, I'll give you peace,
sweet as honey, and its lovely taste
will revitalize your body, soul, and spirit.
Oh yes, rest.

MATTHEW 11:29-30; JOHN 14:27; TITUS 3:5-7;
2 JOHN 1:3

August 18

The grass withers, the flower fades,
but My Word stands forever.
My Word is eternal
and stands firm in heaven and on earth.
My Word is a magnitude of light
that enters you as you read,
and My Spirit pierces
into your mind, soul, and body.
My Word is My glory
in your hands as you absorb,
precept upon precept,
what I have to say to you.
Read. Understand.
I'll do more than guide you;
I'll caress you with the eye-opening embrace
of My wisdom and I'll feed you
with exquisite knowledge of who I am,
and who you are in Me.
My Word is the illumination you need
to travel the path of success
every day.

Isaiah 28:10, 13, 40:8; Psalm 119:89, 105;
Matthew 24:35

August 19

Today, pray for illumination
into My Word so the holy scriptures
will breathe new, fresh life into you,
and infuse your spirit, soul, and body
with understanding, revelation, and healing.
I'll multiply your faith like rain
as you devote time today to the study of My Word.
Treasure this time with Me
more than your daily bread.
My Word is the food
that never leaves you hungry.
Come, and I'll fill your heart like a cup
pressed down and running over with blessings.

Luke 6:38, 21:33; John 6:63; Joshua 1:8;
Jeremiah 15:16

August 20

I see the troubles you're facing–
the problems that leap up
from behind the rise in the road,
the wolf poised to spring forth
to attack your flock
and devour your goods.
Oh, but dear one, you must remember,
whatever comes against you,
contends with *Me!*
Take your power today
and rebuke the devourer. Refuse to accept
the thrashing of the enemy's
spiked tail against the walls of your house
and your life.
Hurl the truth into the atmosphere
and strangle the lie
because your enemy is not flesh and blood.
I tell you, today use the fierce
and undefeatable weapon of *faith*
to combat the source of your troubles.

Isaiah 41:13; 2 Corinthians 2:10:4;
Ephesians 6:12, 16; Matthew 28:20

August 21

You're initiating a new path today,
so before you take your first brave steps,
lavish yourself in the balm of My love.
Breathe the aroma of My love
surrounding you; feel the squeeze of
My embrace, the warmth of
My hand in yours. Let My love ignite
love in your heart, in your eyes,
your voice, your touch.

Listen to the love
I've put in your heart, and trust
where I send you. Trust the task.
Trust the path.
My Spirit has gone ahead for you,
and you need not strive
for a single second. My love carries you
on its wings of sovereign favor.

John 15:19; Deuteronomy 7:8, 13; 2 Timothy 1:7;
Zephaniah 3:17; Psalm 5:12

August 22

Your age doesn't matter, dear one.
Never judge your life's worth
by the constraints of a calendar.
I was thirty years old before
entering My public ministry on earth,
and I ministered just three short years.
When I died on the cross, there were billions of souls
who remained unreached,
untaught,
unhealed,
but the shortness of My life didn't limit My Father.
A moment of time is as a thousand years
in heaven's economy, remember?
I fulfilled My Father's will
unrestrained by the boundaries of time on earth,
and your task is no different.
You will complete the will of My Father for your life.
Fix your heart to Mine.
Love Me.
This is what matters.

PSALMS 39:5, 89:47, 90:4, 103:24;
PHILIPPIANS 2:8; JOHN 14:21

August 23

If you eat at a sumptuous banquet of delights,
or if you nibble on the floor at tasteless crumbs–
when you eat, eat for Me.
If you drink exotic elixirs from golden goblets
reserved for kings, or if you lap water cupped in your hand–
when you drink, drink for Me.
Whatever you do:
If you sleep til the noon sun bakes your bed,
or if you rise up early before the dew;
if you work around the clock, earning little except
the joy of your labor; if you dance with the moon,
sing with the stars; if you bring soup to the sick,
and grain to the poor; *whatever you do, do for Me.*
Work, play, laugh, cry–
love Me–
first.

1 Corinthians 10:31; Romans 14:4-8;
Matthew 22:37

August 24

Imagine the great cities of the world
in all their lighted splendor–
suddenly gone black.
The cities of the world may lose their light,
but not you.
You, My child, are the light of the world.
You're a city set on a hill
that can't be hid.
My Holy Spirit fills and ignites you,
and your light permeates
the spiritual atmosphere around you.
Everywhere you step your foot, you bring
My presence with you,
for I am the light of the world.
Demons hate the light and run screaming.
Walk with the authority of the Light.

Matthew 5:14-16; Psalm 43:3; Acts 13:47;
Philippians 2:14-16; John 8:12

August 25

Today,
I want you to touch
the velvet crest of dawn
in the simple clasp
of a loved one's hand.
I want you to demonstrate your love
to those nearest you
with patience, thoughtfulness,
warmth, and prayer
even though you don't believe
they deserve it.
I expect this of you.
They need you.

1 Peter 1:22; Ephesians 4:32; John 15:12-14, 17

August 26

I'm holding you in the hollow of My hand,
and here in this very private place
where no harm can touch you
you're *home.*
Rest here in the safety of My hand
completely covered, nestled securely.
You can fall asleep here,
and I'll fill your dreams with peace.

Did you know–to rest in My hand
is the longing of all humankind?
The human quest for love and safety
is a cry for *Me.*
My hand is open to you, dear child.
There's no safer, happier place than here with Me–
sheltered and completely loved.

Isaiah 49:16; John 10:28; Psalm 91:1-2

August 27

Live the winged life, beloved,
above the cares that rob your soul of flight.
Fly today! Soar to your waiting joys!
No longer count the scars,
but instead count the prayers I'm answering.
Come to My Word today;
wash yourself in My words of love.
How tender is the wound?
Let Me dress it for you. I'll clean out the infection
and apply My lovely salve of healing
to rejuvenate what's been damaged.
I'll pour on you the warm oil of My Spirit
to renew your strength. Be brave, dear one,
all shiny-clean and strong,
fire up your wings of faith and fly!
Your scars are the tail wind
to propel you higher.

PSALMS 55:6, 103:5, 107:20; ISAIAH 40:31, 53:5;
JEREMIAH 30:17

August 28

The key to being happy when you feel depressed
is to praise Me.
Praise Me in silence and in awe.
Praise Me in thankful whispers.
Praise Me in noise.
Praise Me with instruments,
banners, and flags.
Praise Me with your creative gifts.

Look, I've opened My holy gates for you!
Enter as though you're leading
a long procession of jeweled and robed saints.
Pass the tall carved pillars
along the golden promenade,
and enter My sacred courts
with thanksgiving and more praise.
My house loves dancing, singing, and gladness.
Your praise fills My heart.

PSALMS 33:2-3, 47:5-7, 51:15, 100:1-5

August 29

When you're distressed
and feeling dejected,
what should you do?
I say sing!
When the chains of disappointment
nip into the flesh of your heart,
and you're wilted with ennui,
give us a song! Yes, sing!
I've shown you that the turmoil of life
can't defeat you,
so come, sit on My shoulders,
and sing to Me.
The song of the dark hour of the soul
is significant, just as a rose after its bloom
is significant. The earth tries to devour you
with its sorrows, but I tell you, rise higher;
a new day is coming!
Feel it!
Sing through the forest of disappointment;
sing to the birthing of new things.
Sing, I say. Sing!

Psalms 40:3, 42:8, 104:33; Isaiah 42:10

August 30

Don't be afraid of the trials.
Oh, they'll come at you,
sometimes like arrows raining from the sky.
Trials strike without warning,
landing with multiple hits.
I tell you
get out of the rain; run to your battle station,
stand fast; hold your position!
Strike back; take the offensive!
Never retreat; fight the battle!
I'm your strength in the rumpus.
I give you power to overcome,
and I give you a holy army of helpers.
You have all the help you need.

1 Peter 1:13; Revelation 3:11; Galatians 5:1;
Isaiah 41:10; Psalms 27:1, 91:11-12

August 31

You're oh so worried about the future, My child,
and worry is like a driving rain
beating down on a lone blossoming flower.
Soon the torrent will bow down the head
of the bloom, its fragrance crushed,
and the precious flower becomes
wilted,
soggy,
frayed,
and depressed.
Your storm of worry is not
engineered by Me.
Won't you end this tempest?

If you struggle to manipulate life's eventualities,
your efforts will frazzle you with worry
because you can't control the future.
You *know* the mind of Christ,
but you can't *control* the mind of Christ.
Leave tomorrow to Me, dear one,
and live for *today*.

Matthew 6:27; Philippians 4:6; Isaiah 4:6;
Luke 12:32; Proverbs 16:2

SEPTEMBER

God is able to provide you with every blessing in abundance, so that by always having enough of everything, you may share abundantly in every good work.

2 CORINTHIANS 9:8, NRSV

September 1

The day you were born is an important day.
When I considered your birth,
I took into account the lives of those
whose world you'd share,
so I sent you to take your place among them,
and to live your days for Me.
I purposefully gave you the life you have
in order to fulfill the plans
I personally designed for you
in the world as you found it.
You were born perfectly on time.
I decreed the very day, hour, and moment
when you'd enter life on earth–
tiny, blinking, and wet. Can you still hear the angels
and the welcome song they sang over you?
My Father kissed you on the nose
and said, "It is good."
Honor who you are in this hour.

PSALM 22:9-10; ECCLESIASTES 3:2; ISAIAH 43:7;
PROVERBS 10:9

September 2

Awake, dear one,
and put on your robe of courage–
the beautiful gift I gave you
from My loving Father.
Wear your robe of courage
as you go forth into this day,
and take wisdom as your escort.
Courage and wisdom are powerful
weapons against the devil
who continually tries to bully you.
You need courage and wisdom
to stand against the devil, to stay strong
and not become prey to your emotions.
Wear your robe of courage and
hold tight the hand of wisdom.
Your eyes will be opened.
Your mind will bristle with insight,
and your spirit will be fortified.

ROMANS 13:11; DEUTERONOMY 31:6; PROVERBS 4:7;
EPHESIANS 6:11; 1 PETER 5:8; PSALMS 31:24, 32:8;
JEREMIAH 15:20

September 3

How heavy is your burden today?
Can you, beneath the weight
of your own troubles, help to lighten
the weary load of someone else?
Can you put your complaints on pause
for a moment?
You're never too boggled with care
that you can't help someone else.
You're never too lame to lift up one
who needs a hand.
You're never too blind to help another
see their proper path.
When the hurdles and obstacles
in your life numb you
to the omnipresence of
My loving kindness,
try showing love
to someone.

GALATIANS 6:2; JUDE 1:22-23; EPHESIANS 4:32;
ROMANS 12:10; MATTHEW 5:7; HEBREWS 13:2

September 4

At times your head may hang low
and your shoulders slump
like bags of laundry–
the weight of the world
is too heavy for you to tote!
I tell you,
look for the good in your life.
You're surrounded by My goodness.
My Father loves you
and is *good* to you.

No need to haul the world around
on your back.
Your life is centered in a glowing sphere
of heavenly *goodness*.
Look up and see your personal blessings.
I'm good to you.
In sweetness and in sorrow,
I'm good to you.
In life and in death,
I'm good to you.
Through every trial of the world,
see the good.

Nahum 1:7; Psalms 34:8, 100:5, 145:9;
John 3:16; 1Samuel 2:8

September 5

Do you realize the power you have in Me?
You possess *unlimited* power when
you exercise your faith in who I am in you.
You honor Me and demonstrate
My authority in human lives and events
by confidently and assuredly
exercising your faith in Me.
Faith can only expand with use.
When things are difficult
your faith becomes a living illustration
of My power and grace.
Your faith can be as small as a mustard seed,
and it's sufficient to rattle mountains.
Today, put your faith to use as never before.
Enjoy the leading of My will
and pray the impossible.
Move mountains!

MATTHEW 9:29, 17:20; JAMES 2:17; JOHN 6:28-29;
HEBREWS 2:4, 11:6

September 6

A heart of stone has no pulse,
and a person without compassion
has forged for himself a heart of stone.
Compassion is at the center
of My merciful heart.
Compassion doesn't repel or ignore
the inconvenient and messy needs of others.
Compassion doesn't turn sour
when things go awry. Compassion is never rude,
never judges harshly,
is never quick to condemn,
and is *always* loving.
A person without compassion is like a well
without water–a river of dust.
To be without compassion is to be
rotted fruit shriveled in sand.
You're called and chosen of Me, holy and beloved;
be compassionate in your choices today.

COLOSSIANS 3:12-13; MATTHEW 9:36, 25:35-40

September 7

Come away with Me today,

and let's laugh and be free.

I'm offering you spiritual refreshment.

Let Me hug you with contentment

and a lovely sense of well-being.

Be My carefree child,

and let's go outside and play!

I not only love

the work you do in My name,

I love your recreation, too.

Think of taking time to play as a gift to Me,

and play with all your heart!

I delight in everything about you.

EXODUS 33:14; MATTHEW 11:28;
PSALMS 18:19, 128:2; 1 TIMOTHY 6:6

September 8

Your body depends on you
to care for its needs.
You say, "But ,"bodily exercise profits little.'"
You quote Me wrongly.
Without exercise, you can't prosper
because your neglected body
will hobble along trying to keep up
with your enlightened spirit
and your rekindled soul. Weak and unused,
it shifts into neutral and goes stagnant.
Dear child, your body is your real estate.
It's home for your soul and spirit,
and you can't rent space elsewhere.
It's My Holy Spirit's temple.
Some live to glorify their body,
but I tell you to glorify Me *in* your body.

1 CORINTHIANS 6:19; 1 TIMOTHY 4:8;
COLOSSIANS 2:23

September 9

Don't be timid.
Today, bare your teeth
with grace, clench those fists
with love, and become
a sudden storm of godly authority.
Don't be intimidated
when jealous demons
with fingers like thorns
try to snap up your blessings.
Don't bargain with these devils,
or make a cowering effort to placate them.
Resist and stand against them!
When you're led by My Holy Spirit,
you can't be friends with the devil.
I realize you want to be nice to everyone,
but you can't pacify the destroyer
who wants to slap your soul to hell.
To function wholly and triumphant
in My kingdom, take off your shyness costume
with all the smiley faces,
and put on the My full armor
like the tough, smart warrior
I created you to be.

ISAIAH 59:19; JAMES 4:7; 2 CORINTHIANS 10:4;
EPHESIANS 6:11-12

September 10

Today, I'm giving you extra doses
of grace and wisdom
which you need.
Don't allow feelings of inadequacy to visit you
for one moment.
There's not a believer on the crust of the earth
who's inadequate for the tasks I assign.

You need grace to have the courage to relinquish
your jungle of responsibilities to Me.
Spiritually, you're empowered for greatness!
Don't surrender your glorious power in Me
for a sack of cheesy self-doubt.
I'm accomplishing My purpose in you,
and the choices you face today
depend on your brave, wise frame of mind.
Grace will bring you a caravan of rewards
when you least expect it.

James 1:5-6; Proverbs 2:6; John 1:17;
2 Peter 3:18; Romans 8:28

September 11

When there's hardship
in your life, and your day
isn't going well, don't think
I'm the one throwing
sticks at the spokes of your wheels.
I'm not responsible
if things fall apart and don't go
as you planned.
I'm not evil.
I'm the goodness out of which
flows all goodness.
I'm the fountain of mercy
from which flows all mercy.
I am love.
Don't assign human suffering
as My perfect will.
Don't think I'm the one who
initiates poverty, disease,
destruction, failure, loss,
and misery of every stripe
in the world today.
I have come to pour out life
in the world, and life more abundantly!
I'm here to transform human suffering.
I'm here today to transform you.

Luke 18:19; 2 Thessalonians 2:16; Psalms 52:11, 84:11; John 10:10; 2 Corinthians 9:8; Romans 12:2

September 12

I realize your need for light
at the end of a seemingly endless, execrable tunnel,
but remember I go before you
to furrow out a clean, clear route to follow.
Don't think you're alone.
All I ask is you stay with Me,
close enough to feel My breath.

I'm leading you safely past dark
detours of temptation and doubt.
I'm showing you how to press on
in spite of foul air and emotional mudslides.
I'm leading you across fallen plans and
dashed hopes.
I'm preparing you for a new tomorrow
bathed in the Sonlight of My perfect plan,
and when you step your darling foot
on the threshold of your new life,
there'll be much celebration.

Psalms 27:1, 139:10-11; Romans 6:4, 13:12;
Exodus 33:14; Jeremiah 29:11; Zephaniah 3:17

September 13

Today, walk in the Spirit,
so you won't become entangled
in fleshy stuff of futile worldliness.
In order to stay vitally close to Me
and experience the myriad benefits I offer,
set your soul like a clock
and come to My throne more often.
Come with praise and gratitude;
come with your beautiful love and your faith.

Worship Me along with the legions of angels
who know that praise
is the fountain from which flow
all of My blessings.
You can beg and bargain,
but My holy ears respond to *faith*,
and faith burgeons when nourished
and trained by loving worship.
Set your soul like a clock and come to Me
knowing who I am,
and watch My favor explode over you.

PSALMS 22:25-27, 29:2, 95:6; JOHN 4:24;
REVELATION 7:11; ISAIAH 6:3; HEBREWS 10:23;
DEUTERONOMY 28:2

September 14

Set your affections on things *above*,
and don't get side-tracked
by the racket you hear from below–
in the basement of life.
It's loud down there with the screaming
and yelling of your name.
I'm telling you, get on the
Holy Spirit elevator at once!
Groveling around in the dank,
window-less lower floors of life ruins your eyes.
You get snapped up in noise,
feeling your way around, blinded and stupid.
I'm up here in the holy penthouse!
The *top* floor. There's a rooftop garden
of delights up here, sweet, succulent,
happy, peace-fed.
Where are you?

COLOSSIANS 3:1-2

September 15

Don't ever, for an instant, doubt Me.
I see all and I know all.
Today, I'm showing you more of the mysteries
of My kingdom.
Open the eyes of your spirit and listen with
your spiritual ears because
My ways are not a puzzle for humans to solve,
but a way of life that transports peace,
love, and joy into the human heart.
The hidden mystery I speak of isn't
revealed in the world but is embedded in heavenly
and divine power and wisdom.
If you continue to look for answers to what
concerns you in the breadbasket of the world,
you'll eat, but you won't be satisfied.
I've come to satisfy the longing soul,
to bring joy to the hapless,
hope to the wounded,
and inspiration to the thinker.
I've come with a banquet of mysteries explained
for you to feast on today.
Come and dine.

PSALMS 16:11, 90:14; 2 TIMOTHY 1:9;
1 CORINTHIANS 4:20; PROVERBS 2:2;
REVELATION 3:20; SONG OF SONGS 2:4

September 16

Human eyes haven't seen, nor have human ears heard,
and in fact, it hasn't even entered the heart
of any human being
the things I've prepared for My own
who love Me.
My Spirit searches the depths,
and the only way to know Me
is to be one with Me.
Toss out the icons of other gods. They are distortions
and powerless, pulp and mush.

Dear one, you haven't received the spirit of the world,
but the Spirit from Me!
I search all things, and *I know all things.*
I'm revealing My heart to you
and I really want you to listen.
I want you to know the things
that have been freely given to you by Me.
I want you to know more
than you thought possible to know.

1 Corinthians 2:9-12; Romans 8:27; Leviticus 19:4;
Isaiah 44:9; Matthew 11:27;
Mark 4:11; John 15:15

September 17

Allow Me to slip My hand
beneath your burden and lift it from you.
My love for you is of such intensity
that it's impossible to escape My watchful eye.
I'm glued to you.
We experience life together, dear one.
I'm not parked in a heavenly ramp
while you motor around down in the world on your own.
No no no. *I am with you always!*
You're precious to Me,
and those you love are precious to Me.
What concerns you concerns Me!
But remember, there's no fear in love,
and what frightens you escapes Me entirely.
I fear nothing

Child, you and I are *one* in the Spirit,
so if I fear nothing and I am all-knowing,
and all-powerful,
and present everywhere at once,
what are you upset about?
Pray in My name to dump the fear and the hassled mind.
Love Me and live!
I have wonderful things in store for you today.

Matthew 11:30; 1 Peter 5:7; 1 John 4:13, 18;
Ephesians 6:18; Galatians 2:20

September 18

Listen. The move of My Spirit is like the roar
of the wind.
Evidence of My presence is all around you
and in you.
I've heard your prayers in the wind of My Spirit.
Your loving, gracious heart
has touched Mine;
our discussions have been recorded
and honored.
I'm fulfilling My Word in you today,
and blessings, like rain rushing to the earth,
are coming to you.
Take heart.

Acts 2:2; Psalms 5:12, 66:3, 91:15, 145:18;
Deuteronomy 5:24; Isaiah 1:18; Jeremiah 9:24

September 19

Your choppy travels in self-gratification
have been derailed.
The folly train must stop
at the depot of discipline to refuel today.
Pause to look carefully into
the depot's mirror of My Holy Spirit.
Whose eye winks back at you?
Is it your own, outlined in pouting shadows?
Or is it the sweet reflection of
My Spirit in you?
To be content with your life's circumstances,
you need discipline.
I don't pamper you like damaged royalty.
I don't spoil you by catering to your many demands.
No, I build you–I form character and strength in you!
You'll never be happy without discipline.
I'm at the door of the depot of discipline,
welcoming you for your refueling.

ACTS 13:52; 1 TIMOTHY 6:6; PROVERBS 29:1;
1 CORINTHIANS 11:28; HEBREWS 12:7-11

September 20

I know what you have need of.
I'm concerned about every hair
on your head.
You're concerned about such things as
what to fill your closet with,
and you lust for items in store windows
and on the pages of slick magazines.
You burden yourself with bills
to pay for the things you've bought
that make yourself feel richer
than you are.
Consider the lilies of the field, My love;
they neither toil nor spin,
and they're arrayed in outrageous beauty.
King Solomon, the richest king
in all the world, didn't wear clothing as beautiful
as a single lily.
You're concerned about clothing your body.
What about the wardrobe of your soul?

LUKE 12:27; MATTHEW 10:30-31; ECCLESIASTES 5:11

September 21

Don't be intimidated because
you lack knowledge in My Word.
Not to worry.
I'm speaking directly
to your heart today,
so you'll marvel at the reality
of My presence over you.
Sense the presence of goodness,
peacefulness, answered prayer,
and a Savior who loves you!
Though frustration has been
a constant irritant,
and you've felt inadequate in the past,
I don't want you to be intimidated
by those feelings any longer.
Come to My Word and absorb
into your heart the confidence and assurance
I freely offer you.
Let Me remove the fragments of uncertainty
because a vibrant connection with Me dispels negativism.
Don't worry. I understand you.

PROVERBS 2:6; 18:15; PSALMS 16:11, 42:8; ACTS 2:28;
HEBREWS 9:24; JOHN 1:12, 14:18, 15:16

September 22

Always think of yourself
as a person of integrity–
a person who doesn't rely
on false pretenses.
You've no need to boast
or lie or fumble
with false inventions
to earn acceptance
or keep the peace.
Your integrity
doesn't muff responsibility
but delights in being loyal.
Words embroidered with flattery
and dishonest intentions
make an ugly pattern
to be kept hidden
in the cabinet of mistakes.
This is behavior you avoid.
I love honesty and faithfulness;
I love the wholesomeness and
the incorruptibility of your soul.

PROVERBS 10:9, 19:1; ROMANS 8:10; PSALM 66:16

September 23

Listen to your own words.

Can you hear the tedious grinding

when you complain?

When you complain, it's

living as a shadow scratching around

in the dark without substance.

Your grumblings are shadows and smoke.

They'll vanish in the light of My Word.

Take truth. Take substance. Take heart.

Take the blows. Take wisdom. Take the pain.

Take life!

Honor this day, beloved. Live it fully and cherish it

for everything it brings–everything.

Take the present with all it renders no matter what.

Live the present with all your wisdom, courage and

compassion.

Love the present with the magnificent power of your faith.

PSALM 55:2; NUMBERS 11:1; DEUTERONOMY 31:6,
33:27; PHILIPPIANS 4:11-13; ROMANS 5:3;
2 CORINTHIANS 1:3; PROVERBS 2:6; HEBREWS 11:1

September 24

I know the betrayal you've suffered,

and I know how hard you've tried

to hide from your fears of being hurt again.

Dear one, let Me remove

the fragments of your wounded spirit.

You can face your fears!

In the humility of My love

and in the power of My Spirit,

proclaim the ascendancy of My Word

over your life

to permit the peace that has been stolen from you

to be restored.

True to My Word, *I restore your soul.*

I'll make you a beacon of honor,

but I need you to do your part,

so rise up and wash yourself

in the mist of glorious victory today.

PSALM 23:3; JOEL 2:25; ZECHARIAH 9:12;
1 CORINTHIANS 15:57

September 25

My hand is upon you today.
Don't be discouraged or dejected.
You'll profit much this whole week if you
don't allow yourself to get faint-hearted
and droopy.
I'm revealing Myself
and My creativity to you
in exciting new ways.
I have a few new skies for you to fly,
steep valleys to zip-line across,
tall hills to climb–
and oh, you're going to love these challenges
because you'll see My hand on everything you touch,
and you'll bring My joy with you
wherever you go. I love you.

Romans 12:12; Galatians 6:9; 2 Corinthians 9:8;
1 Peter 1:13; Jeremiah 31:3

September 26

Respect comes with a price.

Honor isn't free of charge.

Integrity is earned.

Those who strut about

with puffed up chests and noses pointed

like silos in the sky

will always annoy you.

You'll never make friends with

the proud unless you bend down to their

base status, and you could hurt

your knees squatting so low;

you could scrape your chin.

Forget about it.

Let the proud bury the proud.

You, dear one, walk with dignity

and humility and be glad

you're free.

2 Timothy 3:2-4; Psalm 40:4; Romans 6:17-18;
1 Peter 5:5-6

September 27

Know My mind.
I'm greater than what you own.
I'm more than all your wants.
You can gather to yourself things–
cars, houses, trips, real estate, investments,
jewels, gold, and silver;
you may own castles in a few countries;
you may have avenues and islands
named for you;
but oh, beloved,
these things don't mean you're rich.
Detach yourself from what you own
and what you don't own.
See yourself as rising tall
above possessions, and be like a pillar of light,
rich in the glory of *My* unlimited resources.
In Me you have no lack
no matter what your bank account says.
I want you to enter the place
where your heart is free
and your mind is at peace,
the place of unending *spiritual* riches.

PHILIPPIANS 4:18-19; PROVERBS 10:22;
COLOSSIANS 3:2; PSALM 49:6-7, 16-19

September 28

There's no place in your life for mediocrity.
Nothing about Me is inconspicuous
or lackluster; nothing about Me is secretive,
lukewarm, or wishy-washy.
If you bear My name,
you can't walk in the world unnoticed;
you can't live a tepid, bland life because
you'll never be invisible.
I am a holy, all powerful, omnipotent God,
and as My child you're on the earth
reflecting Me and the vastness of My personality.
Open your ears
and let Me speak to and through you.
Obey Me fully.
I'm not calling you to be a clanging bell,
a brassy symbol, a loud-mouth bore,
and religious threat, no.
It's our *relationship* that can be seen by all.
There's no substitute for My love for you,
and there's no substitute for your love for Me.
This in itself makes you and your faith
eternally unique.

Psalm 48:14; Deuteronomy 5:24; 1 Corinthians 13;
Revelation 3:16

September 29

Wisdom wants to be your partner in life.
Wisdom wants to preserve your days
and give you good sense, perspicacity, balance.
Wisdom wants to make you discerning
and savvy.
Wisdom wants to teach you how beautiful
your life is, and how honored you are to be called
to live by faith.
Wisdom won't allow you to lament or pine away
for what's not yours,
and wisdom will show you that I made both
prosperity and adversity for your benefit.
Wisdom wants you to have My mind
and be glad.
Today, take wisdom by the hand
and don't let go.

PROVERBS 1:1-7, 4:7, 9:10, 17:24; JAMES 1:5

September 30

I tell you the truth;

your life is good,

and I'll always help you

through the storms of the world

as well as the storms of your mind.

I'll lift you out of every oppressive whirlwind,

and self-destruction will not be your master.

When you're weary, I'll pick you up in My arms.

I'll make you strong and put a new song in your throat.

Be at peace with yesterday

and look at the hope of *today*.

Beloved, look around you!

See the spring of life.

All is new, fresh. All is possible,

all is ours.

Song of Songs 2:10-13; Psalms 39:7, 107:28-29;
3 John 1:2; Romans 9:17

OCTOBER

"I have loved you, my people,
with an everlasting love.
With unfailing love I have
drawn you to myself."

JEREMIAH 31:3, NLT

October 1

I want you to climb into the arms
of My goodness for this new month.
I want you to snuggle into the safety
of My love and mercy
and feel totally secure in My nourishing care.
I'm creating new passageways leading you
into the holy chambers of My heart.
Wisdom and knowledge are your lighted beacons,
I tell you, and the joy of life is yours.
I don't mislead and I don't lie.
I want you tucked in My sweet embrace
eating the fruit of contentment under My watchful gaze.
Oh, take what I have for you today!
Treasure these words.
All that I have is yours.

PSALMS 31:19-21, 36:7-9; NUMBERS 23:19;
HEBREWS 6:17-18; PROVERBS 2:6-7; LUKE 12:32

October 2

In the past you've looked to people
for approval.
You compared yourself with others
and were snared
in the unstable notions
of inferiority and superiority.
I put you on the earth to be a star
in My kingdom and to glorify Me.
When you put Me first,
and your ways please Me,
I'll make even your enemies
to be at peace with you.
Put Me first today and you'll experience My favor
to accomplish your calling
with dignity and success.

Job 10:12; 1 Peter 1:23; Proverbs 16:7; Psalm 33:9;
Ecclesiastes 10:10

October 3

Can you stop comparing yourself
with others and start living
for *My* approval?
Oh the blessings and delights
that wait for you!
Here with Me you'll discover
lasting joy–the kind that doesn't up
and evaporate at the first whisper
of an emotional drought or heat wave.
The joy I give you disdains
the behavior of fair-weather friends
and the hollow physiognomy
of fake heroes.
When you discover
your own immense value to Me,
you'll stop comparing yourself
with others and start believing in
the person I've created you to be.
Your confidence will inspire and draw
many to Me.

Acts 10:34-35; James 2:5; 2 Corinthians 10:12;
Psalms 32:3, 107:9, 118:18; Hebrews 10:35

October 4

Dear one, I'm here.
I reach into your need eagerly!
Swiftly!
Like pulling a rabbit from a snare,
I'm here to free you from the hunter's trap.
I see all the dangers you're unaware of;
I see the traps set in wait,
yet your foot won't be seized between their teeth
because My promise to keep you safe
is iron-clad and hewn in solid rock.
Stay close to Me. I'm your fierce,
protective barrier against all dangers.
I'm here to show you how to maneuver
the quick-tempered tsunamis when they hit.
The missiles of doubt, anger, and fear
hurtling everywhere won't hit you
when you're in My arms.

PSALMS 68:19, 91:1-14; HEBREWS 6:17-18;
2 THESSALONIANS 3:3; 2 CORINTHIANS 1:20

October 5

When your anxious thoughts multiply in you
like mice chasing crumbs,
and when your week is consumed
with the polluted air of worry and doubt,
pause for a moment and look for Me.
Can you find Me
in the nighttime of your mind?
Your gnawing fear is more deadly
than the serpent's fangs,
more menacing than
the hungry lion on the hunt.
Your anxious thoughts are thieves
meant to slam you,
to bruise and break your dignity.
Don't give fear another minute.
It's the call of the jackal,
the drool of the sluggard.
Be brave!
There's never been a saint without sorrow,
never been a hero without impediments.
Today, trample the venom of fear
and take your place of strength and honor with Me.

PSALMS 27:1, 3, 91:13, 94:19, 100:1-4;
2 TIMOTHY 1:7; 1 JOHN 4:18; HEBREWS 13:6

October 6

You've been waiting for answers to prayer,
and you've been patient.
Don't let doubt bite you on the neck
when you've come this far trusting Me.
Doubt will strip you of your faith
simple as peeling an orange.
I told you I would never leave you,
and above the shouts of confusion
know that I'm here with you as you wait.
I'm answering you–
but in *My* time.
Let Me carry you to the place
that is *best* for you.
Let Me bring the *best* to you.
Let Me multiply My *best* for you.
Isn't the *best* worth waiting for?
Endure a little longer, dear one.
Endure with triumph.

James 1:3-4, 5:16; John 15:7; Psalm 27:14;
Hebrews 6:14; Acts 20:32; 1 Corinthians 2:9

October 7

Today is the day
for you to take your place
in My divinely appointed school of the brave.
Today is the day to take your seat
and be strong and confident in who you are!
As an initiate in the school of the brave,
you'll no longer be able to mope and grovel unprepared
for weekly tests, probes, and exams.
You won't be permitted to oversleep
with no light to guide you to the moment of truth
where you rise up victorious against fear and shame.
Here in the school of the brave you'll
value your gifts while singing the school song,
Let the weak say I am strong!

NAHUM 1:7; 1 CORINTHIANS 16:13; JOHN 14:1;
HEBREWS 4:14-16; PSALM 119:11; EPHESIANS 6:10-11, 16;
JUDE 1:24-25; 2 CHRONICLES 15:7; JOEL 3:10

October 8

Fear of the future is a deadly enemy with nothing
but vapors as ammunition. It insults your
spiritual integrity to worry about the future
when I AM your future.
No pestilence will overtake you in spite of
your worries and fears.
I've given you abundant life to appreciate and be grateful for!
Open your heart and mind
to receive the wonders of it.
Pause today and meditate on "abundant life" and what
this means to you at this moment.
Consider the hours, days, and years ahead,
then see them spilling over with abundance,
with blessing,
with prosperity,
with love,
with joyfulness.
It's all yours.

1 John 4:18; Psalms 9:10-11, 23:4-5; Isaiah 12:2;
2 Corinthians 8:7

October 9

Today, I'm empowering you
to resist the temptation
to return to your old ways of thinking.
I'm empowering you to renounce
self-pity and self-aggrandizing
because your heart
was meant to soar freely
with exuberant joyfulness!
Don't let yourself flip-flop back into
the dialogue of demons with dreary,
depressing self-talk that squashes out faith
and happiness, slamming shut the blinds
on the glorious panorama of My creative plan for you.
Poor me is not an expression
heaven recognizes.
Snap open the blinds of truth today
and shut up those ungodly thoughts.
Why allow your best to be captured
and your strengths paralyzed?
You're My faith-child;
tell yourself the *truth.*

PROVERBS 23:7; EPHESIANS 3:14-16, 4:23-24, 5:8;
JOHN 8:32

October 10

When you look only for blessings
and answered prayers
as the assurance of My love,
you limit your experience of Me.
My gift to you is the full vocabulary
of life's poetry.
My gift is all life's literature,
even the discordant phrases
and passages that are difficult and tragic.

When your prayers and desires
are centered only on worldly blessings and rewards,
and not Me,
discouragement will become your buddy.
I'm here to give you the full measure of life's gifts,
but understand that trials can be gifts.
They're meant to change you to become brighter,
more beautiful, and more like *Me*.
Can you be as content with life and its stony paths
as you are with sunshine and flowers?
The greatest gifts I've given you are the ones
you carry within you!

James 1:2-3; Psalm 71:1-2; Matthew 7:11;
Philippians 4:11; John 14:26; Ephesians 1:13;
Acts 2:4

October 11

Do the work I've called you to do today.

Be brave, be strong!

Pull down the strongholds.

Fight the good fight.

Resist the devil.

Power is yours.

Wisdom is yours.

Courage is yours.

Peace that passes understanding

is yours.

Let Me be the loving guide and friend

who enables you in everything

you're called to do today.

Observe with the mind of Christ,

and in every word you speak

and all you do,

let Me be the inspiration.

PSALMS 119:11, 143:10; PHILIPPIANS 4:7, 13;
EPHESIANS 6:10; 1 CORINTHIANS 16:13-14;
2 CORINTHIANS 2:16, 9:6-8

October 12

In the Prayer I modeled for you,
I taught you to pray for
deliverance from evil. The evil
I want you to think about today
is your own tendency to agree with,
and team up with, the devil
who is the master of evil.
There's not a human being without
the tendency to sin, so I'm telling you today
to be aware and on the alert
for your own desire to slither backward
into such traps as jealousy, greediness,
and a critical spirit.

I've given you Holy Spirit power
to transform each nettled nest of discord in your heart
into a clean, polished, welcoming home for Me.
Look into your heart now.
I promise to relieve and deliver you from everything
you acknowledge and confess to Me.

MATTHEW 6:9-13

October 13

Don't ever assume I'm the cause
of your temptation to sin.
I *never* lead you into temptation to sin.
I don't come at you with urgings
of wrongdoings. Never!
I want you to understand that temptation
and testing are two different things.
Abraham was not led by *temptation* to offer
his son, Isaac, as a sacrifice to Me.
He was *tested with the test of obedience*,
to refine and build his faith, and he was therefore
hugely blessed.

The test of obedience is not the same as temptation to sin.
The *devil* tempts you to sin.
I set you free from sin!
I'll initiate tests of faith to strengthen and draw you
closer to Me. I want you empowered with wisdom,
courage, and inner fortitude. I want you
to rise up with character, dignity, and genuine godliness.
Trust Me.

Matthew 6:13; Hebrews 11:17; James 1:3,
1 Corinthians 10:13; 1 Timothy 3:16, 6:11

October 14

Never stop praying!
But I want you to understand that
your prayers can be hindered by an attitude
that's more self-centered than Me-centered.
No human being is entitled to take credit
for answered prayer.
Answered prayers are *Mine*.
It's not a *person* who answers prayer and performs
the miracles, it's *Me!*

Place the desires of your heart inside the desires of My heart
and lift them up to Me.
Pray *believing* I'll answer.
When your fervent, faith-rich prayers
are funded with love's currency,
I'll send My answers zinging into your holy mail box
like gold lightning.

John 15:7; Matthew 21:22; James 5:16;
1 Thessalonians 5:17; Mark 11:24; Hebrews 4:16;
Psalm 145:18-19

October 15

I want you to see Me quietly caring
for the hurting, the desperate, and the poor.
I want you to see that nothing escapes My eye.
No hurt is too trivial and no dilemma too small
to command My care.
I'm the God of kings, and I'm the God
of the sparrows and lilies.
Hannah of old prayed for years
for a son. I heard her the first time, of course,
but I answered in My time, not Hannah's.
She didn't give up, but continued to cry out to Me
because her will and Mine were *one*.
She wanted what I wanted!
Hannah lifted up My desire with her own,
and ultimately, her prayer was for My honor.
We both wanted a son for her,
and the prayer was answered.
Her story, and the birth of Samuel,
is to encourage you to search your heart for My heart
when you pray, and to not give up.
Trust My purpose, trust My caring,
and trust My timing.

MATTHEW 5:3; LUKE 6:20; 1 SAMUEL 1:20;
PSALMS 31:15, 103:17; 1 PETER 5:7

October 16

I won't let you fall,

don't worry.

I've always been here to hold you up

to guide and protect you,

and I'll *always* be here. I'm not eons away

out in space; I'm *in* you.

Yes, I hold your hand, but I also hold your heart.

If I'm *in* you that means by your choice,

you can fuse your thoughts with Mine.

Your dreams, your longings, your passions,

are not separate from Mine when we're one.

Today, I want you to transcend

from the worldly grip on your life that comes and goes

like a moth beating at the window.

Be fixed to *Me* and we'll fly together

to your divine destination.

Isaiah 40:28, 31; 2 Corinthians 4:18;
Philippians 4:13; Hebrews 7:26

October 17

You're precious to Me;
never forget that.
Never lose sight of these sheltering words.
I am fully aware of each facet of your
character. I know your choices,
your strengths, your flaws, and your glories.
I know you better than you know yourself.
Your aims in life are too low, however,
and your target unfocused.
This is why your confidence is shallow.
Open your eyes of understanding today,
and stop permitting the clouds of sin
and self-reproach to waste your energy.
I give you your breath,
and I number your days.
Take charge of your choices today,
and make Me Lord of absolutely
everything.

ROMANS 8:35-36; JEREMIAH 31:3; PSALM 90:12;
JOB 14:5; 1 JOHN 1:9

October 18

I know you're in need of help,
and I'm answering you,
but first
I want you to see yourself
as *one* with Me. We aren't separate and apart.
You aren't stationed on terra firma while I'm
up the clouds with a pair of holy binoculars and
a yellow legal pad taking notes.
Understand that My Spirit is *in* you.
We're united from *inside*;
are you listening? I'm here now!
We're spiritually connected
in a divine, miraculous fusion making us *one spirit*.
What's born of the flesh is flesh,
but My Spirit fused with your human spirit
has created a new life in you.
Right now. Here and now. This minute.
When you ask for My guidance, don't fancy Me
yanking your sleeve or holding onto your foot
yelling, "This way!"
Darling, I'm *in* you. Listen with your *heart*,
and you'll hear Me.

JOHN 3:5-6, 16:13; LUKE 3:16; ACTS 22:14

October 19

You're carrying a heavy burden today,
and you may feel worn out and depressed.
Oh, dear one, I, too, carry a burden,
but My burden is *light*.
Would you like to exchange the heaviness
of your burden
for the lightness of Mine?
When your attachments oppress you
and you feel weighted and over-extended,
come and be yoked with Me
where you'll find rest,
relief,
ease,
and refreshment.
Let Me teach you the easy rhythms of grace.
The lightness of My burden can be yours,
easy to be borne,
comfortable,
blessed
because *together* we can handle anything.

MATTHEW 11:29-30

October 20

You call yourself generous
and so you are.
You're a giver.
You love to give,
and I love it that you love to give.
You give nice things to people.
You shop, buy things,
you send flowers, you remember birthdays.

Today, I want you to remember to give to Me
before you wrap that next present.
When you buy a gift for a person,
think of it as a gift for Me.
Give your greeting cards, your good deeds,
your heart to Me.
If you give because it feels good
and because giving earns attention,
it becomes self-centered giving.
I gave you your giving heart
for Me-centered giving.
Give your gifts to Me first.
I love you.

NUMBERS 18:29; 2 CORINTHIANS 9:7; EXODUS 34:14;
PSALMS 29:2, 95:6; 1 CHRONICLES 16:29

October 21

A gift is measured by the effort and love
it took to give it, and every gift you give wings to
goes to your heavenly savings account
where nothing is calculated by numbers but by
integrity.
I want you to see the divinely appointed
authority of the gifts you give to people.
When you give a gift through effort, grief, sacrifice,
sorrow, hardship ,and joy,
it bears powerful authority.
Start to proclaim the authority of your gifts,
for such gifts aren't mere charitable
niceties; they're kisses from Me!

The gifts you give from a selfless heart
go to Me first, and then to your recipients.
No matter how simple or grand, freely give,
whatever the cost,
because it's the heart of the giver
that multiplies itself
and only what you give from the heart
is truly yours
and Mine.

HEBREWS 6:14; 2 CORINTHIANS 9:15;
PROVERBS 18:16; JOHN 6:9-14; MATTHEW 10:8; 1
CORINTHIANS 2:12; REVELATION 21:6

October 22

The closer we are,
the easier it is for you to accept being loved
by others.
Love is not something you earn.
You're loved because you're flat-out loveable.
I've given you many gifts to share,
and as you fill your heart and mind
with growing closer to Me,
you'll want to reach out
to accept the love of those around you.
They have much to give you.
Truly be, and let yourself be loved.
Fill your whole heart with My words.
Fill your whole mind with My mind.
Fill your body with My enabling health.
Fill your soul with the knowledge of My will.
Dear one, a refreshing new creative spirit
is about to explode in you.

1 John 4:7-8; Ezekiel 36:26; John 17:3;
2 Corinthians 5:17

October 23

Heaven's currency is *love*.
Let's look at your heavenly bank account today.
Have you tallied the expenditures and deposits
made this month in your heavenly bank account?
How much have you drawn out compared to
what you've put in?
You opened your heavenly account with *love*.

Love is more than a human feeling and doing nice deeds–
it's an expression of who I am.
I AM LOVE.
If only you realized how your heavenly account multiplies
and expands when you make regular love deposits.
You store up treasures that multiply and gather interest
each time you make your love deposits.
If only you knew how happy you make all of heaven
when you pour out your love for Me because only then
can you distribute the immensity of your wealth
in loving others.

Deuteronomy 6:5; Joshua 22:5; Zephaniah 3:17;
Matthew 22:37; John 13:34; Romans 12:10, 13:8;
1 Peter 4:8

October 24

I watched a poor widow
place her last two coins into the temple treasury,
and her humble offering
is still honored today as a precious gift—
yet the glamorous gifts of the indifferent rich
of the day are long forgotten.
You're hired as chief financial officer
of My money as it comes to you.
You approve the bills and sign the checks.
How much or how little filters into your hands
is not important. What matters is the dedication
to multiply generosity and faith.
Be an emissary for My kingdom
and assign authority to your gifts and tithes.
Appropriate My money with dignity
from your high position
in My holy banking system.
It's not frugality I honor;
it's wisdom and faith.

MALACHI 3:10; 1 CORINTHIANS 2:12; LUKE 12:48,
21:1-4; MATTHEW 6:21; LUKE 6:38

October 25

Don't be afraid of bad feelings.
Respond to the feelings of your heart
honestly and openly here in the light of My love.
Don't let your irritation and unresolved anger
get stuffed under the bed and behind closed curtains
because anger is a wily devil. It'll turn on you
and punch you until you're its victim.
Come into the light with Me.
Let's see clearly and listen carefully, so
facing your feelings will reveal
what you need to know about yourself.
Know you're loved
and safe. You're empowered
and forgiven. You're on the brink of
something wonderful. Nothing can take you down—
unless you let it.
I give you the power and authority of My name
to cast every evil hindrance out of your life.
Replace the strangling tentacles of anger
with the healing nectar of mercy.
Freedom and peace are yours.

EPHESIANS 4:26; PSALMS 37:8, 91:1; PROVERBS 15:18,
16:32, 19:11; COLOSSIANS 3:8; JOHN 8:36, 14:13

October 26

I know the reasons for your behavior.
You need love, and you long
to be relevant and appreciated.
I want you loved, relevant,
and appreciated too!
I want you to walk in favor.
When your ways please Me, you'll have favor!
(Run off on your own without Me,
and you're a pawn of chance.)
I have greatness ahead for you–
respect, appreciation, love, and relevance–
everything you long for.
It's not in the milk of self-centeredness.

PSALMS 27:1-14, 32:8, 37:23, 119:9, 28;
ISAIAH 40:29; PROVERBS 16:7, 19:21;
EPHESIANS 3:16-17

October 27

You think you're bogged down with a situation
that's impossible to get out of, but I'm here to crank open
the lid of the box and set you free.
I can work miracles in your life if you'll let Me.
You can stop fretting and scratching your chin with worry.
My name is Deliverer. My name is Healer.
I'm in you by My Spirit, and I am guiding you by My Spirit,
turning things around for you, opening pathways
to set you free. I'm your divine physician.
Don't concern yourself with sins of the past. You're forgiven.
I've forgotten the things you keep mentioning.
If you've been foolish, remember I've told you
that the foolish will confound the wise, so sanctify your heart
and make it beautiful in Me!
Let Me cauterize the situation. Let Me be the miracle worker,
and you...you proclaim My authority and power,
and be My trusting child.

MATTHEW 17:20; LUKE 1:37; ROMANS 6:6;
PSALMS 32:8, 73:24; ISAIAH 58:11; JOHN 16:13;
HEBREWS 2:4; 2 CORINTHIANS 5:7

October 28

Today, put out of your mind the wrongs others have done to you.
The evil-doing of others has no power over you
unless you foolishly give them that power.
Resentment will lead you to futility and misery,
and I'm telling you, don't squander another moment
on what you can't change.
It's time to push the offenses
out of the cupboard of your beautiful mind
because bitterness kills
like rats ravaging a dung heap.
Bitterness will shut you off
from the Sonlight of My Spirit
and make you a prisoner in your own head.

I'm asking you to trust Me
to bring new and fabulous blessings
into your life.
I want you to humbly rely on Me
so you can face the calamities you've endured
with courage, no longer traumatized,
but with holy confidence and perfect peace.

Matthew 6:12, 14-15; Isaiah 38:17; Ephesians 4:31;
Hebrews 12:15; Romans 8:38-39

October 29

I'm calling My seasoned generals out of seclusion,
calling them out into the heat of My final battle.
I'm calling My seasoned veterans who worry they're too old–
out of their quietude,
out of their repressed jobs in the back yards of the young
and ambitious,
out of their backseats
and basement positions in the churches,
out of their gratuitous jobs
and unsung ministries.
I'm calling My seasoned veterans
into the forefront of My 21st century campaign
to shift the atmosphere of the entire planet.
Be ready!

Zechariah 10:5; Isaiah 64:4; Hebrews 10:23;
Psalms 18:39, 31:3, 48:14; 1 Corinthians 14:8;
Nahum 2:1

October 30

Here at My holy beauty spa,
where life makeovers are the specialty,
I'm doing a great work.
The treatment begins with My calling you
out of darkness, and then with a gentle heave-ho
you're placed in the hot room
of My glorious light where you see yourself
for who you are.
Do you need the total Holy Spirit makeover today?
First, the amazing cleansing process
purifying the pores of the soul, a complete
body-soul spirit bath where you dump your sins
and foibles down the condemnation drain and emerge
golden in forgiveness.
Don't let old-fleshy yesterday keep you from
your divinely appointed, healthy new-life look today.
I am Jesus. I love you,
and here at My holy beauty spa,
I work miracles.

1 Peter 3:3-4; Hebrews 4:16; Romans 6:4;
Ephesians 2:4; 2 Corinthians 5:17

October 31

All heaven is behind your success.
The words I speak create life
and power, so today, take My Word
as your authority,
your strength, your shield, and your oxygen.
If you'll see truth in all that I tell you,
your faith will intensify, and your success will
burgeon beyond human ability
to the point where you'll bring to pass that which is not
by contending and speaking it out.
Haven't I told you whatever you ask in My name
I'll answer?
Isn't it written that faith is the substance
of things *unseen?*
In Me you have the good success I ordained
for you from the beginning.

JOSHUA 1:8-9; HEBREWS 4:12, 11:1; PROVERBS 1:23;
MARK 11:24; PSALM 40:5

NOVEMBER

Taste and see that the LORD is good;

blessed is the one who takes

refuge in him.

November 1

You were born at an exact perfect moment in time.
I called you into being
for such a time as this.
I have every one of your days before
My eyes.
Each moment and each breath
is important to Me.
There are no mistakes on heaven's holy calendar,
so today, I'm calling you to be grateful
and to honor the days and months and weeks and hours
and minutes
I've given you
in the world.
Your life is always before Me.
Cherish the moments as holy events.
Cherish today.

ESTHER 4:14; PSALMS 17:2, 34:1, 37:23;
COLOSSIANS 3:4; 1 PETER 1:23-25, 2:9

November 2

Heaven rejoiced at your birth,
and rejoiced again when you gave
your heart to Me.
Angels sing at the altar
of the repentant heart.
I'm your shield, your glory,
the one who lifts your head.
Listen for My voice today.
I'm leading you in a new path,
and you'll hear Me in the stillness
and in the quietness of your mind.
Hinge your thoughts
to My gentle guidance.
Can you feel My kiss on your forehead?

LUKE 1:79, 12:8, 15:7,10; PSALM 23:1-2; LUKE 1:79;
PHILIPPIANS 4:7; JOHN 16:27

November 3

Be good to yourself today.
Be tender-hearted, kind, and merciful
toward yourself as I am merciful to you.
The wrongs done to you have hurt and angered you,
and I know you've suffered.
I tell you, darling one, these afflictions will produce
an eternal weight of glory if you let Me
take your hand and lead you to inner freedom.
You have the power to forgive within you,
and when you forgive,
the sins done against you lose their prominence
on the walls of your memory,
and the stains on your heart will evaporate.
I don't want you to go on hurting and
giving the devil your time and attention.
Forgive and be free. The pain is temporary;
the glory is eternal. Let the glory rise within you.
Be good to yourself.
Forgive them.
Forgive yourself.
Forgive life.

EPHESIANS 4:31-32; 2 CORINTHIANS 2:10, 4:17-19;
PSALM 119:50; 1 PETER 1:8, 5:11

November 4

I'm the author of love
and its rule on earth.
All creation was formed by love.
When you absorb yourself in My love,
vibrating with its intensity,
you then begin to exude love back to Me
and the world around you.
This is the life force between us–you and Me–
a power greater than anything on earth.
It's the essence of eternity.
Today, allow your love to be pure and selfless,
and make every effort
to give and receive with a generous heart.
Your single purpose
is to love and be loved by Me.
I delight in you.

1 Corinthians 13:13; 1 Peter 4:8;
1 John 2:5,10, 15, 3:11, 23, 4:8-9, 11, 16, 19

November 5

So many decisions.
Shall you go this way or that?
Shall you go left or right? With this one or that one?
Oh, what should you do?
When in the valley of decision
and you can't seem to find direction,
too often your decisions are based on
what you think will make you happy
and what will be most advantageous for *you*–
and later, when you're eating the bitter fruit of your choices,
choking on the bad taste, you'll blame Me
for not stopping you.
Haven't you learned by now?
The valley of decision is a test
to ponder what would be best
for you and Me both.
Ask yourself what would honor
My kingdom?
That which honors Me will always
honor you.

Joel 3:14; Joshua 24:15; 1 Samuel 2:30;
Revelation 4:11

November 6

When you leave Me out of your plans and decisions,
I don't interfere. I'm very considerate.
If you choose to lie down with dogs
in the mud holes of life, you're free to do it.
If you choose to chomp on contaminated meat,
I won't stop you.
I didn't jump in shouting protests at Adam and Eve,
"Stop right there, you two! Put that apple down!"
did I?
They had, as you do, the gift of choice.

I gave you the gift of free choice not
to do whatever you want to do;
I gave you the gift to choose to obey Me
and do what is good in My eyes.
I gave you free choice to make glorious,
earth-shaking decisions to bless and make beautiful
your world.
Today, you have choices to make.
What will you do?

DEUTERONOMY 11:26-28, 30:5; 2 CORINTHIANS 9:15;
JEREMIAH 7:23; ACTS 5:29

November 7

Did I create the apple
for its own sake?
Did I create the sweet peach
to bless itself?
The rose?
The pineapple?
The fig?
No, I created these for *you*.
Within each fruit are seeds that multiply more
of its kind, and so it is with the gifts I've given you.
My Holy Spirit lives in you as the supernatural
kernel of life that generates more of Myself
so the world might be blessed through you.
There's never been a peach
plucked from a tree for its own sake.
And you, darling, alive and thriving
from My tree of life, bearing the beautiful savor of heaven,
are multiplying more of Me right now.
Right where you are.

GENESIS 1:11, 26-28, 9:3, 17:2; EZEKIEL 17:8, 47:12;
MATTHEW 3:8; JOHN 15:2

November 8

Dear one,

greatness is My job, not yours.

I ask only for your love.

Works without love mean little to Me.

Do you remember reading about

My encounter with the Samaritan woman

at the well at Sychar?

I was thirsty and the dear woman not only gave Me water,

but at My words, she arose in a flutter of praise and love.

What about you? I'm thirsty for your *love*.

Before you fast and sacrifice your goods to Me,

check the purpose.

My living flame transforms

your soul into the very soul of love.

It's who I am.

Today, walk in your own flutter of praise and love.

Deuteronomy 6:5; John 4:7-42, 14:23;
Psalms 16:2, 103:1-5

November 9

When you need a physical healing,
come and gaze intently at the cross
where I bore your sicknesses and your sins.
In My Word I've told you
that you'd know the truth
and the truth would make you a free person.
Hug these words to your heart today–
Truth = Free.

Fully open yourself to receive what I've told you.
Think about, believe, and love the truth
that sets you free from your physical ailments
and every adverse entanglement you encounter.
Proclaim My Word to be true
to your beautiful body.
Love your body as I do,
and be healed.

MATTHEW 8:17; 1 PETER 2:24; JOHN 8:32;
PSALM 103:3

November 10

Today, I want you to see how precious
your body is to Me.
I've told you that My Word is life to you
and health to your whole body.
This means I love your *entire being*,
no matter what shape,
size, age, or condition.
Soak yourself in this truth.
Put this truth on as a coat. Swallow it as fruit.
*My Word is life and health
to your body.*
Today, absorb what I'm telling you.
Set aside time in your schedule
to find My words of healing and health,
and make them yours.
Yours!
I'm the LORD who invigorates, heals,
restores, and renews your youth like the eagle's.
Believe this today, and honor your body.

PROVERBS 4:20-22; PSALM 103:1-5; EXODUS 15:26;
JEREMIAH 31:17

November 11

Don't underestimate the relevance
of your tears.
I've gathered and counted each one, My darling.
My heart is large enough
to hold your hurts.
I'm with you in lack, in plenty, in joy, and in sorrow;
I'm with you in tears and in laughter—good and bad.
You may be tempted to think that affliction
comes from Me, but I have not treated you badly.
I don't afflict you. I save you!
I never turn My head when danger comes your way,
though you may not sense My presence.
I don't leave you when things go wrong in your life,
nor can My love for you waver for an instant.
I catch your tears in My hand,
and turn each one to diamonds for your crown.

JOHN 14:27; 1 CORINTHIANS 1:9; HEBREWS 13:8;
REVELATION 21:4, 7

November 12

If you lose your way,
you can always count on Me
to come find you.
Heaven's holy taxi service
will be right there to transport you
where you belong.
Your home is in the very specific center
of My will, My dear,
one with Me, sound and found.
With Me you'll glow with health,
your bones vibrating with life.
But off-course without a map
you become shaky, unstable;
you can't see the way.
Oh, dear one, don't wait for a second.
Call heaven's holy taxi service
and I'll bring you right home.

PROVERBS 3:5-8; PSALM 91:1; HEBREWS 4:16

November 13

I'll never let you bake in the oven
of your mistakes.
If you've taken some wrong paths
and gotten yourself tangled
in relationships you'd like to get out of,
I'm here to help.
I have plans for you—plans to prosper you and
to open doors of possibility.
So come to Me openly,
honestly, and let's make a new start.

I'll remove the hot glare from your life,
and I'll place you in your sweet destiny.
Put your faith in Me.
Be strong and trust Me.

PSALM 103:3-4; JEREMIAH 29:11; PHILIPPIANS 1:6;
PROVERBS 3:5-6

November 14

Don't doubt your faith, My child.
Doubt your doubts.
Your feelings and emotions aren't
reliable sources for you to base
important decisions on. In Me you have
the guidance you need
because I have the plan for your life.
I've numbered the hairs
on your dear head. I've calculated
the breaths you've breathed
and stored them in golden containers
to celebrate a life being lived
for *Me*.
You are close
to My heart.
Never doubt My love. Never doubt
who you are in Me.
Make your decisions with Me.

MATTHEW 10:30, 14:31; JAMES 1:6; JOHN 16:33;
PSALM 25:9; ISAIAH 58:11; 2 CORINTHIANS 5:17

November 15

My power is working in you
mightily today.
My Word has made you alive,
and the power of heaven is right now
yanking you up out of the muck
of the world and its mess of temptations.
Darling, you're going to experience victory
over the situation you've been going through.
Begin to think of the problem as dissolved.
Be relieved.
Set your dear foot on your new path
with glad expectation.

PSALM 119:43, 50; JOHN 8:36; PROVERBS 30:5

November 16

Pause for a moment, take a deep breath,
allow your shoulders to relax,
and be still.
Let the following words reach into your
heart and mind:
The righteous shall flourish as the palm tree.
Palm trees live long, dear one.
Many species live over a hundred years.
The palm tree flourishes happily
producing fruit in its season and is
a source of beauty to the world.
My child, you are beautiful to Me,
and your days are in My hands.
Take another deep breath
as you bring the word *flourish*
into your heart and mind.
Now, gently and sweetly,
close your eyes and believe.
Today, flourish.

PSALMS 46:10, 92:12-14

November 17

There's a time for all things.
Keep yourself, My love
and you'll understand.
You can't live in self-absorbed flesh
and at the same time be available
to My Spirit.
Today, set a deliberate choice of your will
to obey My Word, to worship Me,
and to walk in wisdom.
Take authority over your choices
and set your heart on the greatness of My
wisdom and knowledge.
I know what you're up against.
Your clever strategies without Me
will tire you out. Can you trust
My will for your life today?

PROVERBS 4:5; JOHN 6:63;
PSALM 95:6; JUDE 1:20-21

November 18

When the fury of life and the fears of the day
get to you and cause your throat to tighten,
your stomach to flinch,
listen for the song I'm singing to you.
Be very still and hear the music,
more luscious than human ears can bear.
Honey-smooth and fragrant
is My love song to you.
Shudder with joy at the melody
inside the noise of the storm around you
and rest your wonderful self in Me.

Isaiah 30:30; 2 Thessalonians 1:7; Romans 5:5;
Zephaniah 3:17

November 19

It pleases Me
when you refuse to allow your ego
to be the central moving force in your life.
It pleases Me when you don't stress
over the trifling opinions of others.
Wisdom has shown you to stop
driving yourself to impress the world.
I'm pleased when you zap your lust
for approval and rest in *My* love and approval.
I delight in you when you tell Me
the life you're living now is no longer all about you,
and you're living by faith in *Me!*
Willingly I gave My life for you
to see you vibrate with glory
and to hear you speak these words to Me.

GALATIANS 2:20

November 20

Eyes stuck to the world and its fickle rewards
will confuse you and make it difficult
to repent, change, and gloriously move forward.
If you crave pleasure and are driven to
escape discomfort, avoid pain,
and narcotize hurtful memories,
you'll be blinded to the blessings
I have for you of spiritual strength.
Dear one, it takes courage to be truly happy,
and temporary pleasures will never
satisfy you. I want to give you a clear mind today,
like gazing out a clean window.
want you to be brave and face the world
with all its trials and unpleasantness,
but look for *goodness and mercy*.
Goodness and mercy are right there in plain sight.

1 CORINTHIANS 2:12; PSALM 33:6

November 21

Open your spiritual ears,
and listen to the gold-toned nectar
of perfect harmony that lives in you.
Listen for heaven's voices in concert,
open wide your wonderful heart,
and sing along.
Angels' voices are lifted up in praise
for their Creator.
They're singing a song of happiness.
They're making the beautiful music of
love, joy, peace,
patience, kindness, goodness
gentleness, faithfulness, self-control–
Will you sing along?

ZECHARIAH 2:10; GALATIANS 5:22-23

November 22

Why do you suppose I told you
that it's more blessed to give than to receive?
Wouldn't you think it would be more blessed
to be on the receiving end?
Oh, but hear Me today.
You *are* on the receiving end when you give!
I want you to grab hold of this principle right now
so you never forget.
When you give from the heart,
directed by Me for My purposes,
you are really *receiving*.
When you give sparingly, worried about your little self
and your little needs, that's exactly what you get back.
Little.
When you give as I give–bountifully, joyfully, richly–
that's exactly what you'll receive in return,
and the bountiful blessing return is yours!
Perhaps the question is, darling, *where* you should give.
There are always those with the palms of their hands
waving at you in the face–so I tell you, *listen to your heart.*
When you're thrilled with the pleasure of giving
there'll be no room for coercion, duty, obligation, or guilt.
Let's give together.

Acts 20:35; 2 Corinthians 9:6-9; Proverbs 11:25

November 23

I don't want you addicted to religious sanctimony
or efforts trying to prove how holy you are.
I don't want My children galloping about
with banners of false righteousness.

I want you to see Me with My arms open
to all of My creation, and especially
to those of My own household.
I want you to understand how precious is
each person and each breath of life.
I want you to be *in love with Me*
and to love one another.
I live in the deep, abiding passion
of eternal, omnipresent *love*,
and I ask you to live in that love too,
because religious addiction will never
love you back.

COLOSSIANS 2:16, 23; LUKE 12:44; PROVERBS 11:9;
MATTHEW 6:5, 23:5; DEUTERONOMY 6:5;
JOHN 13:34-35, 15:13

November 24

When you glue your mind to a thought
or idea, that thought or idea
takes root in you, and whatever is rooted in you
overtakes you, which is why
I've told you to glue your precious mind
to the things that are true, honorable,
just, pure, lovely, kind, and gracious.
Fill your mind with such thoughts,
and they'll grow in you until
they become a part of you.

I want you to think and ponder on the things
of Me, and put an end to the stomping and trampling
of heavy, profane thoughts in your head.
Rebuke your mind's wandering to dark places
and insert *My* mind in you.
You'll grow closer to Me every day,
and you'll experience a beautiful life
of ultimate freedom and peace.

PHILIPPIANS 2:5-8, 4:8; 1 CORINTHIANS 2:16;
PSALM 103:3; 1 PETER 2:14; JEREMIAH 30:17; JOHN 14:27

November 25

Patience, My child, be patient.
You're an important part of My great eternal plan,
and not as an almost-winner, or as a once-was
or as a coulda-been, you're *it*.
You're the right-now, in-the-game, authentic child of Mine.
I've sent you out with My anointing and blessing
to practice My presence everywhere and in all things.
Conquer frustration.
Accept the time that real achievement takes.
Make patience your friend. Be ready for anything.
Today, think about finding happiness
as you wait. Persevere in the upward climb–
in the struggle and the thankless hours.
Let your soul expand and grow,
not squirming out of problems
as frustration would have you do.
I want you strong in character,
and complete in Me.
Suffering is a portion of triumph.
Remember that.

MATTHEW 16:26; JAMES 1:2-3

November 26

When you're alone and uninterrupted,
you have the holy privilege to see yourself
with clear, honest eyes minus all outside influence.
Don't be afraid to spend time alone.
Alone you have the opportunity to listen to yourself
and to carefully observe the way you're living.
It takes daring and boldness to pull down the veil
of neutrality and take a good, piercing look
at yourself in the light of My Word.
Do you see yourself continually captivated by Me?
Have you brought Me into all situations?
All activities? All relationships?

2 CORINTHIANS 13:5; PSALM 26:2; ROMANS 8:6-8;
GALATIANS 6:8; 2 TIMOTHY 2:4, 22

November 27

Each new day I give you
the opportunity to drink from the fountain of joy
and to flourish like a prize-budding rose.
I don't want you to lie gasping
on the blistered ground of yesterday.

Pick up the pieces of your life
and take a good look at them.
Where does each one belong?
Should any pieces be thrown away?
Which pieces will you repair?
Where are the pieces that fit
perfectly together?
You're not in the mouth of a drought.
The worst is never the worst.
I've called you to flourish
with every piece of your life in place.

Ecclesiastes 7:8; Job 14:7-9; Psalm 42:11;
Jeremiah 31:17; Proverbs 11:28

November 28

I'm preparing a banquet of wondrous treats
for your beautiful soul today.
Come and have a feast with *Me*–
feast on our friendship.
Experience the delight of a refreshed soul.

I want you to recognize your need for joy.
When you groan with spiritual hunger
and feed yourself with earthly foods,
bread, wine, gooey stuff, sweets,
empty chatter, and entertainments–
you'll stay hungry.
You can't *fully* live without My perfect joy
flowing in your veins.
I died on the cross to give you the gift of My joy.
Today, let's
be joyful *together*.

PROVERBS 15:15, 17:22; NEHEMIAH 8:10; PSALM 100:1

November 29

I treasure your faith.
Your faith in Me is built on love,
and it's monumental enough
to move mountains,
heal the sick,
bring hope to the hopeless,
and give courage to the feeble.
From faith springs every good thing,
giving the authority to overcome evil
and to charter unknown seas.
Without faith it's impossible to please Me.
I want you to understand the immensity
of one miniscule mustard seed of faith.
Understand that one beautiful act of faith in Me
has the power
to change the course of human history.

HEBREWS 11:6; JOHN 6:28-29, 14:12; GALATIANS 6:9;
1 JOHN 5:4; MATTHEW 17:20

November 30

My Spirit, the life giver,
breathes new spark into your endeavors today,
and produces fresh vitality into what was
asleep. You're being blessed with freedom
to accomplish new things. Arise, shine,
for your light has come!
My glory is all over you.
You're radiant!
Oh, what a day this is!
Joy, the mother of enthusiasm,
fills you.
Arise I say,
and go ahead, dear one, shine!

SONG OF SONGS 2:13; JOHN 6:63; ISAIAH 60:1

DECEMBER

"I have said these things to you, that in
me you may have peace. In the world you
will have tribulation. But take heart;
I have overcome the world."

JOHN 16:33, ESV

December 1

You're on a fabulous journey, dear one,
so don't get frustrated.
This intruder, frustration, will cause you
to grab for immediate rewards,
will yank you down a slippery hill
to avoid the slow, steady upward climb
of the unpaved highway I've set you on.
When you encounter difficulties,
the nasty blubbering of frustration
takes over your thoughts
and it's time to pay a visit
to My Holy Spirit's traveler's aid station
for sweet rejuvenation.
My Spirit will show you
that the challenge of the roughest path
on life's sojourn, the one
few people choose,
is by far the most rewarding.

PHILIPPIANS 3:14

December 2

Is there a problem too great
that My Word doesn't cover?
Is there a situation I can't handle?
Did I leave something out when I laid the
foundation of the earth?
Did I forget something when I took your
sins, burdens, and cares on My body
on the cross?
My child, I hear your complaints
and your grievances, but you're forgetting
I'm bigger than they are.
Cast your cares upon Me, I tell you,
it's of no advantage to complain
when you can pray and proclaim with confidence
that I am the strength
of your life.
Today, gather your fears and doubts in one heap,
deposit them at the foot of the cross,
and proclaim the victorious power of My Word
over every situation you face.

1 Peter 5:7; Joshua 23:14; Job 15:11;
Isaiah 55:10-11, 58:11; 2 Corinthians 1:20;
Psalm 33:9; Proverbs 30:5

December 3

I hear you when you say
you don't have enough time to do everything
you think you must get done.
Would you like to know the truth of the matter?
I'll tell you if you listen.
You've been afraid of self-denial, of saying no
to yourself; you're afraid of not being appreciated,
of disappointing someone; you're afraid of failure, of being
unimportant, of being out-done.
The problem is not lack of time, dear one,
it's lack of discipline.
There *are* enough hours in the day.
I'm here to give you a heavenly boost
and a divine nudge to help you recognize
your need for discipline and sustained dedication to a task.
I never give you more than you can handle.
There is nothing to fear.
I've given you the ability to do all things well!

Galatians 5:24; Hebrews 12:11; James 1:6;
Colossians 3:23; Ecclesiastes 9:10;
Philippians 4:13

December 4

You want to climb a mountain today,
but have you considered
that I may be asking you
to *descend* the mountain?
Have you considered
that I may be waiting for you
down below in the valley of humility?
Your strength is in *humility*
not in your conquests.
You aren't the master,
I am.
The valley of humility is a place
of glory and honor.
It's a place where you see who I am
and who you are in Me.

PROVERBS 15:33, 18:12, 22:4; EXODUS 3:14;
PSALMS 107:9, 139:23; JAMES 4:10

December 5

Pray for My strength to rise up in you

and overtake your inclinations

to act according to your *feelings.*

My servant Peter depended on

the fervor of his feelings

instead of relying solely upon

My supernatural strength and courage,

so he sank in the stormy water

when he could have walked without a problem.

You're stronger than you think,

and you have boundless courage in you.

Reach inside and draw out

more of the power of My Spirit

to meet your needs, help others,

and walk on your stormy waters.

MATTHEW 14:28-30; PSALMS 27:1, 86:7; ACTS 4:31;
1 CORINTHIANS 4:20; ZECHARIAH 4:6;
ROMANS 8:38, 9:17, 15:13; NAHUM 2:1

December 6

If you feel empty and drained of energy,

I understand.

I'm here.

I'm here to revive you.

My Spirit is in you to lift you up

and restore your soul

to an even happier and more energetic you.

When you're weary and without

strength to carry on, take a deep breath,

fix your thoughts on Me,

and let Me love you.

When you feel you have nothing to give,

give Me that nothing.

Hebrews 12:12; Psalms 23:3, 40:5, 139:7;
Galatians 6:9; Ephesians 1:11-14, 17;
Proverbs 16:3

December 7

When you're caught up in your dizzying plans,
demanding projects, and driving goals,
eventually you'll find yourself frazzled
and wondering why you can't
seem to manage your life without stress.

I don't want you to wear yourself out doing good work;
I want you to celebrate the *process*.
I want you to be energized by your
conversations with Me, so your creative
gifts will unfold and flower.

Notice how your energy is spent. Notice
where and when you find yourself
drained and exhausted.
Notice where and when you're happy
and joyfully alive.
Notice where you need to make
some changes.

ISAIAH 40:31; ROMANS 6:11; JOSHUA 1:7; AMOS 5:4;
MARK 2:17; ACTS 3:19; DEUTERONOMY 28:3-6

December 8

You'll love what you know
when you love the truth.
When you act according to what you love,
you become like the truth you love.
Think about it.
You were created for more truth
than you can carry in your natural mind,
and you were created for much more love
than you reach for.
If your only reality is confined within
the impulses of your human nature,
your identity can't soar higher than your limitations.
You're stuck!
Today, realize your entire identity
rests in Me.
I want you to enter
your gorgeous, fully-formed identity,
mounted and framed in the truth.
I want you fully alive in *Me* today
as you've always been meant to be.

JOHN 8:32; DEUTERONOMY 32:4; ISAIAH 16:5;
PSALM 73:26; COLOSSIANS 2:9-10; ROMANS 8:11

December 9

Have the courage today
to live as I meant you to live.
Have the courage today to partner with Me
for your beautiful life.
Your true being is in Me.
Allow Me to convert your shrunken world
for My vast, endless eternity.
Allow Me to convert your selfish human will
to the glories of Mine.
Your struggle against temptation
divides you against yourself
with conflicting loyalties and
and wants.
I'm calling you to enter your true identity,
the one I formed before you were
in your mother's womb.
I called you, named you, and loved you
from the moment I first thought of you.

JOSHUA 1:7-9; 1 PETER 2:21; 1 JOHN 2:6;
HEBREWS 12:2-3; PSALMS 22:10, 139:13

December 10

Don't be upset at that thorn in your side.

I'll pull it out.

In the meantime, be glad

that the power within you

is greater than any struggle or hassle

on the surface and surrounding you.

A thorn is not a sword. An annoyance and nuisance

is not a catastrophe (though it may feel like it).

I'll cause the voice of My authority to be heard.

The majesty of My voice and the strength of My arm

will be known!

My voice will carve flames of fire

in the conscience of all opposition to My will.

Be still and trust Me.

2 Corinthians 12:7; Ephesians 6:12;
Psalms 29:5-9, 46:10; Proverbs 30:5;
John 8:9; 1 Timothy 4:2

December 11

I'm peeling from you the unnecessary
and the banal.
I'm pouring My thoughts into you.
I'm climbing upon the pinnacles
of your finest hours.
Listen.
My voice shakes the wilderness–
your wilderness.
This is a new day for you and a time
to increase!
Be glad and expand the pegs of your tents.
I'm going to cause
your good deeds to multiply.

PSALMS 3:3, 29:8, 139:17; 1 CHRONICLES 4:10;
GENESIS 1:28

December 12

Receive all you have as a gift from Me,
and honor what you have.
I especially want you to respect the currency
I entrust to you, even if it's less than you desire.
Gain understanding and financial integrity,
and allow Me to prosper you *My* way.
If you're given to whim and an urge to possess things,
you'll clutter up your destiny.
I'm watching what you do with My gifts.
One piece of gold or one million are the same to Me.
Both require prudence and conscious management
to multiply and do good for My kingdom.
Humility multiplies riches,
but ignorance will diminish My blessings.

Isaiah 55:2; 2 Chronicles 26:5;
1 Timothy 3:3, 6:10; Proverbs 10:22, 11:25.
Psalm 112:3; 1 Corinthians 12:1

December 13

When it seems everything is against you,
and you don't think anyone's listening
to you; when the world around you collapses
at your doorway in heaps of nasty insults
and contention,
that's the precious moment to turn to Me–
to dive into Me, hang on tight,
and don't let go. Cling! Hold on!
When you feel like you're in the pits,
I'm in there with you.
Wrap yourself around Me;
I'll pull you out.

Isaiah 41:13; Psalms 35:24-28, 40:2

December 14

I know your soul,

and I know how to restore your soul.

If you're weary,

disappointed, or bored,

I know what will perk you up.

When you need a holy lightning jolt

of energy and creative breath,

immerse yourself in things you love.

Take Me with you and listen to good music,

read a great book, work out, go for a walk, dance.

Fully engage in what is beautiful and

inspiring to your thirsty soul.

Be restored as a holy lightning jolt

of love and peace overtake you and lead you

to peace, new energy, and inspiration.

I'm with you.

Psalms 23:3, 51:12; Isaiah 2:5; Ecclesiastes 3:1-4;
2 Corinthians 12:9-10; Colossians 3:3

December 15

Today, seize the opportunities I've placed before you
because when I make a promise to you.
My words aren't mere sounds or nice platitudes;
each syllable is breathed from My holy mouth
ordained to reach and teach you.
You'll succeed because I've said so.
My words over you are forever
settled in heaven!
My words infuse you with ability
that can't be counterfeited.
You'll succeed at your task
as I have planned it.
I'll never let you plunge headlong
into collapse.
When you believe and trust Me,
you become a golden thread
in the fabric of My perfect will.
There's no higher calling.

1 Peter 1:25; Jeremiah 15:16; Ezekiel 12:25;
Psalm 119:89; Hebrews 10:36

December 16

All that lives, moves.
The smallest microbe throbs, pulses, breathes.
A bird of flight, a deer running,
a skittering insect–
leaves in trees bristle and flutter,
then shiver and float to the earth.
Clouds jostle the landscape of the sky,
and the wind shakes like
restless fringes across the earth.
All that lives moves,
but *fear* paralyzes,
turns the bones stiff and the breath stale.

My soul takes no pleasure
in the one who shrinks back, benumbed
and deadened with fear
because I've given you the power and courage
to be free, to move!
Will you kick your fears
into the caravan of My love now?
I can't guide and motivate you
if you're not moving.

Colossians 3:10; Hebrews 10:38, 1 John 4:18;
2 Timothy 1:7; Psalm 27:1-3; Deuteronomy 3:16;
Joshua 1:9

December 17

You're worried that your hard work
might not produce the results you desire.
You're worried you'll lose precious time,
and you wish you could see into the portals of tomorrow
to be positively certain you'll succeed.
Such thoughts form mushy lakes in your head,
your feet become buried in weeds,
your dreams wander like smoke.
Awake I say!
No energy spent in My kingdom is wasted.
No time is ever lost in a labor of love.
My rewards aren't temporary fireworks.
I'm forever!
I bless your soul.
I enrich your heart.
I kiss your spirit.
Listen to Me: you'll succeed
as you invest in a life of faith
trusting that I'll do through you
My good pleasure.

EPHESIANS 5:16-17; PROVERBS 10:16,
12:25; PHILIPPIANS 4:6-7; 2 JOHN 1:8;
ECCLESIASTES 10:10; 1 JOHN 3:18-20; LUKE 12:32

December 18

Today, I'm drawing more creativity out of you.
Dip into the source
of all that is life-inspiring,
and be My mind and My heart.
Discover joy in sorrow,
create beauty out of ashes,
learn strength through weakness,
make something wonderful out of nothing.

Find the music in the storm,
see the colors of a thousand rainbows
in confusion's murky gray.

Consider life's simple treasures
to fill your home.
Multiply blessings, and prosper
in the adventure of loving.
All that you do in love
will create more love.
Discover this and
see how truly creative
you are.

Isaiah 40:29, 61:3; Romans 4:17; Job 26:12;
2 Corinthians 8:7; John 15:16

December 19

Walk in your integrity today.
Walk with Me.
Iron sharpens iron,
and I am the friend who sharpens you.
I draw from the depth of you
where I've planted strength
for every purpose.
I've given you a heart
to recognize, understand
and be acquainted with My ways.
I'm your *best* friend.
Your whole heart fits within Mine.
Your soul is knit with Mine,
making your presence a gift to the world
and a joy to Me.

PROVERBS 18:24, 19:1, 27:17; JEREMIAH 24:7;
PSALM 119:63; JOHN 15:12-14

December 20

I don't send sickness on you
as punishment or to get
your attention.
I'm in the business of *healing lives.*
I'm your healer and deliverer.
I command My healing
and it's done.
I want you to understand that I know
what I'm doing, and that
no matter what you see or hear,
be a mighty prayer warrior.
As My child,
you have authority to decree
and proclaim My Word, and I want you
to focus your heart and mind
on what I've taught you of redemptive
healing. *Take your authority*
and proclaim My will for healing
and deliverance.
I embrace *all* your needs.

PSALMS 103:3, 107:20; 1 PETER 2:24; JAMES 5:15;
JEREMIAH 30:17

December 21

I'm your future.
I'm removing the struggle.
I'm cleaning you up
from the inside out.
I'm removing old habits and
filling you with a higher vision.
The devil's honey-laced voice
feeds you sweet poison tasty on your palette,
but it's death to your soul.
I'm here to strip the ugly things off you
if you'll let Me.
A full, happy life awaits you—
a future with no more secrets.

GALATIANS 5:1, 19-21; PROVERBS 18:9; LUKE 10:19;
MARK 16:17; 1 JOHN 4:1-4

December 22

I'm standing at the door of your heart
quietly calling.
Hear My voice and open the door.
I'll come in to you,
hold you, and tell you
wondrous things you need to hear today.
We'll share the feast of life together,
you and I,
We'll be one.
Hear Me.
Come to Me.
Open to Me.
Our time together is heaven-blessed
and holy.

Revelation 3:20; John 10:27; Colossians 2:1-3

December 23

Today, in this Christmas season,
you have an opportunity to be generous
and you may be tempted to withhold,
to draw back,
but I tell you, pause and listen to your heart.
If you hold back, a vacuum of loss is created
that blocks My blessings and your joy.
Remember I've said the generous soul will be made rich,
and the one who waters will also be watered.
I'm a giving God, abundantly generous, and it's
My Spirit who lives in you prompting you to give.
Lavish your gifts of love and kindness.
Give these without reservation and with holy generosity.
To live the honored life, don't hesitate
to give your love.

PROVERBS 11:25; PSALM 112:5, 9; EPHESIANS 4:32;
1 JOHN 4:7-8

December 24

How do you feel
knowing that I am the God of the universe,
and I have your destiny in My hands?
Do you have a huge sense of relief and joy
rushing through your veins
as you contemplate how secure,
sheltered, and anchored you are in Me?
Does your heart swell with the velvety goodness
of divine peace flowing into every cell
of your being as you meditate on your elevated
position in the heart and mind of the Almighty?
Are you overcome with genuine love and
holy gratitude knowing all is well?
Are you pleased to know your destiny
is having a wonderful time
in My hands?

HEBREWS 6:19; EPHESIANS 6:24;
PROVERBS 1:33, 2:33; JOB 11:18

December 25

Listen for Me today.
I want you to hear My voice.
Can you describe My voice
like the rush of many waters
over your soul as the King of glory comes in
whispering, chanting, loving?
I'm the voice inside the storm clouds
that paint the sky.
I'm the thundering storms;
I'm the voice in the somber wake
of the earthquake, and I'm the consuming fire
you can't name.
Today, as you celebrate My birth,
listen for My voice.
My voice is great and covers
the entire expanse of the earth;
yet, I speak in a voice hushed and small,
imperceptible to the non-spiritual ear.
I'm the voice in the still garden,
and I'm the voice
walking the hallways of your mind
right now.

EZEKIEL 43:2; PSALMS 18:13, 29:4, 8; MATTHEW 17:5;
GENESIS 3:8; REVELATION 3:20; PROVERBS 8:4

December 26

Before you aim for experiences,
aim for a pure, heroic heart.
Before you chase miracles,
chase a faith-filled life
based on love.
Before you fight for attention,
have faith enough to be quiet.
I'm revealing more of Myself to you
one step at a time.
Your faith will grow from a grain of sand
to a field fit for battle.
Faith multiplies with use,
and faith is at the front line
of all your scrimmages.
Faith is the real hero in your life.

MATTHEW 5:8; 1 CORINTHIANS 13:4-6;
HEBREWS 11: 1, 6; 2 CORINTHIANS 5:7; 1 JOHN 5:4;
ROMANS 1:17; PSALM 18:39

December 27

Today, I'm ushering you into My throne room
where you'll open your spiritual eyes and see
unimaginable glories. You'll see yourself as I see you,
perfect and whole, and shining in My image.
I wash you with My Word and I chasten you
with My holiness.
As you prepare your week remember
where you've been and who you are.
You live in My presence;
you bring Me wherever you go
and into whatever you do.

MATTHEW 8:3; REVELATION 3:21; GENESIS 1:27;
1 CORINTHIANS 15:49; PSALMS 16:11, 140:13

December 28

Be willing to live by My time, not yours
because your works are set
by the holy clock of My perfect timing.
All things happen
in the appropriate time, dear one.
There's a time for laughter
and a time for crying.
There's a time for sorrow
and a time to be carefree.
There's a time for plenty
and a time for lack.
All of time
is in My hands.
Time is designed by Me to serve you.
Fix your agenda according to Mine,
not yours,
and watch how your plans, intentions,
schemes, and systems
will each fall into place finding their
perfect timing.
Today, fix your schedule according
to the holy clock of My perfect timing
and find yourself at peace.

Ecclesiastes 3:1-8; Psalm 62:8; Philippians 4:7;
Isaiah 26:12

December 29

I'm creating a new heart in you.
The sweet ecstasy of union with Me
transforms you–
creates all things new
in you.
I'm elevating you above the thick fog
of vanity,
and I'm setting you free
from the futile pursuit
of seeking your own best.

Ezekiel 18:31; Acts 20:32; Romans 8:16-17;
Ephesians 1:11-14

December 30

I've called you to prosper
in every area of life.
I want you to give and invest in others,
for this is wisdom.
Humility and faith are your banners
and your guides. Goodness and mercy are your
accomplices. Joy and prosperity
are your rewards.
I'm calling you today
to give more of yourself to others.
As the year comes to a close,
consider multiplying your gifts,
and invest in lives as never before.
I'll guide you,
and you'll ride the heights of glory
rejoicing.

2 Chronicles 26:5; Psalms 23:6, 112:3;
Proverbs 10:22, 11:25; Matthew 25:14-29

December 31

I placed a boundary for the sea with sand,
and though the waves of the sea toss and shake,
they can't prevail against the fortress
of simple grains of sand ordained for My purposes.
When your plans and My plans
are united in a single, beautifully ordained divine plan,
no storm will prevail against us.

I know your dreams,
and I'm familiar with your plans.
I hear the daily orchestration of your thoughts.
You have no secrets from Me.
I know all things,
and I want you to know My deep, intricate ways.

I want you to know My omniscience.
Pause now and allow the secrets of your heart
to fall into My compassionate hands
where I can gently hold them.
I have wonderful plans for you,
and at this year's end, let Me supply you with
a new vision.

Be thankful for this departing year and embrace the new.
I'm in all your tomorrows.

Jeremiah 5:22, 29:11, 31:3; Romans 15:13;
Psalms 68:19, 147:11; Acts 1:8; John 14:12; Isaiah 35:1